Dr. Ernst Kris of the New School for Social Research, and Dr. Bertram D. Lewin of the New York Psychoanalytic Institute. The report used multiple sources in profiling Hitler, including informants such as Ernst Hanfstaengl, Hermann Rauschning, Princess Stephanie von Hohenlohe, Gregor Strasser, Friedelinde Wagner and Kurt Ludecke. The work is considered a groundbreaking study and was the pioneer of offender profiling and political psychology, today commonly used by governments when assessing international relations.

(N.S.)

Henry Murray

OCTOBER, 1943

FOREWORD

Aim

The aim of this memorandum is:

1. To present an analysis of Adolf Hitler's personality with a hypothetical formulation of the manner of its development.

2. On the basis of this, to make a few predictions as to his conduct when confronted by the mounting success of the Allies and…

3. To offer some suggestions as to how the U. S, Government might influence his mental condition and behavior - (assuming it sees fit to do so) and how it might deal with him, if he is taken into custody, after Germany's surrender.

The proper interpretation of Hitler's personality is important as a step in understanding the psychology of the typical Nazi, and, since the typical Nazi exhibits a strain that has, (for a long time), been prevalent among Germans - it is a step towards understanding the psychology of the German people.

Hitler's unprecedented appeal, and the elevation of this man to the status of a demi-god, can be

Analysis of the Personality of Adolph Hitler

With Predictions of His Future Behavior

And Suggestions for Dealing with Him

Now and After Germany's Surrender

**Prepared for the OSS
(Office of Strategic Services)**

by Henry A. Murray, MD
Harvard Psychological Clinic

October 1943

Edited and Designed by N.S. for
Kodselim Square
© 2017 All Rights Reserved

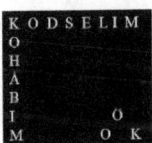

INTRODUCTION

The Analysis of Adolph Hitler, with Predictions of His Future Behavior and Suggestions for Dealing with Him, Now and After Germany's Surrender, was a two-hundred and forty page typewritten manuscript prepared for the wartime OSS, (Office of Strategic Services), by the Harvard Psychology Department under the supervision of Henry A. Murray, MD.

Henry Alexander Murray (May 13, 1893 - June 23, 1988) was an American psychologist who taught for over 30 years at Harvard University. He was Director of the Harvard Psychological Clinic in the School of Arts and Sciences from 1930. He was instrumental in introducing psychoanalysis into the Harvard curriculum and developed a theory of personality called ***PERSONOLOGY*** that is based on "*need*" and "*press*." This theory involves the concepts of *latent needs* (that are not openly displayed); *manifest needs* (that are observed in people's actions); "*press*" (or, external influences on motivation) and "*thema*, that is a pattern of press and need that coalesces around particular interactions. During World War Two he served as Lieutenant Colonel in the Office of Strategic Services.

Analysis of the Personality of Adolph Hitler, was commissioned by the head of the OSS, William, "*Wild Bill*" Donovan. The report was done in collaboration with psychoanalyst Walter C. Langer, explained only on the hypothesis that he and his ideology have, almost exactly, met the needs, longings and sentiments of the majority of Germans.

The attainment of a clear impression of the psychology of the German people is essential if, after surrender, they are to be converted into a peace-loving nation that is willing to take its proper place in a world society.

SOURCES OF INFORMATION FOR THIS ANALYSIS

As is well known, there are no thoroughly reliable sources of information about Hitler's early life, and what is known about him, since 1918, is in many respects insufficient or contradictory.

This analysis has been based, for the most part, on the following materials:

1. Data supplied by the Office of Strategic services.

2. Hitler's **MEIN KAMPF,** New York, Reynal & Hitchcock, 1939.

3. Hitler's **MY NEW ORDER,** New York, Reynal & Hitchcock, 1941.

4. Heiden, K., **HITLER, A BIOGRAPHY,** London 1936.

5. Rauschnnig, H., **VOICE OF DESTRUCTION**, New York

6. Baynes, H. G., **GERMANY POSSESSED,** London, 1941

It is generally agreed that **MEIN KAMPF** is not to be relied on as a factual document, but, as the translators say in the introduction to the American edition; this work "*is probably the best written evidence of the character, the mind and the spirit of Adolf Hitler.*"

SECTION ONE: CONDENSED REVIEW OF THE ENTIRE MEMORANDUM

CONFIDENTIAL MEMORANDUM
CONTAINING

A. Brief Analysis of Hitler's Personality.

B. Predictions of Hitler's Behavior.

C. Suggestions for the Treatment of Hitler.

D. Suggestions for the Treatment of the German People.

Submitted by Henry A. Murray, M.D.
Harvard Psychological Clinic
Cambridge, Massachusetts
Committee for National Morale,
New York.

A. Brief Analysis of Hitler's Personality

I. Dynamical Pattern, Counter-Active Type

There is little disagreement among professional - or even among amateur psychologists - that Hitler's personality is an example of the counter-active type; a type that is marked by intense and stubborn efforts:

1. To overcome early disabilities, weaknesses and humiliations, (wounds to self-esteem), and:

2. Sometimes also by efforts to revenge injuries and insults to pride.

This is achieved by means of an *"Ideal-Ego Reaction Formation"* which involves:

1. The repression and denial of the inferior portions of the self, and;

2. Strivings to become (or to imagine one has become) the exact opposite, represented by an "ideal-ego," (or image of a superior self), successfully accomplishing the once-impossible feats and thereby curing the wounds of pride – and winning general respect, prestige and fame.

This is a very common formula, normal (within limits) and widely admired in Western cultures; but in Hitler's case all the constituent forces of the pattern are compulsively extreme and based on a *weak, neurotic, structural foundation.*

The chief trends are these:

1. Counter-active need for dominance, superiority.

2. Counter-active aggression, revenge.

3. Repression of conscience, compassion and love.

4. Projection of criticize-able elements of the self.

Counter-Active Need for Dominance:

The developmental formula for this is as follows:

1. Intolerable feelings of inferiority (partly because of yielding to the will of a harsh and unjust person) leading to:

2. Contempt of one's own inferior traits (weakness, timidity, submissiveness) and the fixed determination to repress them in oneself and to condemn them in others, accompanied by:

3. Admiration and envy of power in others and a vision of self as ultimately superior (ideal-ego) leading to:

4. Repeated efforts to become superior (counter-action out of wounded pride), encouraged by moments of extreme self-confidence in which one believes oneself the equal of one's vision.

This, as we have said, is a very common form of

development, but in Hitler the trend is so intense, and the commonly balancing forces of affection, conscience, self-criticism and humor are so weak that we are justified in speaking of megalomania (delusions of omnipotence), despite the fact that the man has succeeded in getting a large proportion of the German people to believe that he is superior, that he has been divinely appointed to lead them to power and glory, and, that he is never wrong and hence must be followed with blind obedience, come what may.

Hitler's underlying inferiority feelings, his basic self-contempt, are shown by his choosing, as criteria of superiority – (traits of ideal-ego) – attributes and capacities that are the very opposite of what he is himself or once was.

This may be illustrated by his fervent eulogy of brute strength, purity of blood and fertility.

1. (a) Admiration of Brute Strength - Contempt of Weakness:

Hitler has always worshipped physical force, military conquest and ruthless domination. He has respected, envied and emulated the techniques of power, even when manifested by a hated enemy.

From first to last he has expressed contempt of weakness, indecision, lack of energy, fear of conscience; and yet Hitler has many weaknesses.

There is a large feminine component in his

constitution. As a child he was frail and sickly and emotionally dependent on his mother. He never did any manual work, never engaged in athletics, was turned down as forever unfit for conscription in the Austrian Army. Afraid of his father, his behavior was outwardly submissive and later he was annoyingly subservient to his superior officers.

Four years in the army, he never rose above the rank of Corporal.

At the end he broke down with a war neurosis: hysterical blindness.

Even lately, in all his glory, he suffers frequent emotional collapses in which he yells and weeps. He has nightmares from a bad conscience and he has long spells when energy, confidence and the power of decision abandon him.

Sexually he is a full-fledged masochist.

1. (b) Admiration of Pure Noble German Blood − Contempt of Jewish, Slav and other Blood:

Hitler has always extolled the superior qualities of pure, unmixed and uncorrupted German blood. He admires the aristocracy.

Concurrently he has never ceased expressing his contempt of the lower classes and his aversion to admixtures of the blood of other races - of Jewish blood especially - and yet Hitler's own origins are not noble or beyond reproach.

Hitler comes from illiterate, peasant stock derived from a mixture of races - no pure Germans among them. His father was illegitimate, was married three times, and is said to have been conspicuous for sexual promiscuity.

Hitler's mother was a domestic servant.

It is said that Hitler's father's father was a Jew and it is certain that his godfather was a Jew, and that one of his sisters managed a restaurant for Jewish students in Vienna, and another was, for a time, the mistress of a Jew.

Hitler's appearance, when he wore a long beard during his outcast, Vienna days, was said to be very Jewish.

Of these facts he is evidently ashamed. Unlike Napoleon, he has rejected all of his relations.

As a partial explanation of his complex about impurity of blood it may be said that, as a boy of twelve, Hitler may have been caught engaging in some sexual experiment with a little girl, and later he seems to have developed a *syphilo-phobia*, with a diffuse fear of contamination of the blood through contact with a woman.

It is almost certain that this irrational dread was partly due to the association, in his mind, of sexuality and excretion. He thought of sexual relations as something exceedingly filthy.

1. (c) Advocacy of Fertility

Fertility, the family as the breeding ground of warriors, multiplication of the German race, these have been cardinal points in Hitler's ideology; and yet;

Hitler himself is impotent. He is unmarried and his old acquaintances say that he is incapable of consummating the sexual act in a normal fashion. This infirmity we must recognize as instigation to exorbitant cravings for superiority. Unable to demonstrate male power before a woman, he is impelled to compensate by exhibiting unsurpassed power before men in the world at large.

1. (d) Achievement of Power through Oratory

Hitler could neither change his origins nor decree his potency and, unlike Mussolini, he has never tried to develop himself physically; but he became, for a while, the most powerful individual in the world, primarily by the use of mass-intoxicating words. Aristotle has said that the metaphor is the most potent force on earth, and Hitler, master of crude metaphor, has confirmed the dictum in this generation. By seducing the masses with his eloquence and getting them to accept him as their divinely appointed guide, he compelled the smaller circles of industrialists, politicians and military leaders to fall into line also.

Hitler, speaking before a large audience, is a man possessed; comparable to a primitive medicine man, or shaman. He is the incarnation of the crowds unspoken needs and cravings; and in this sense he has been created, and to a large extent invented by, the people of Germany.

Hitler has Compared the masses to a woman who must be courted with the arts and skills known to passion only, and it is not unlikely that the emotional source of his orgiastic speeches were childhood tantrums by which he successfully appealed to his ever-indulgent mother.

1. (e) Significance of the Counter-Active Pattern

Counter-Action is essential to the development of strength, but in Hitler's case it has been extravagant and frantic. He has not ascended step-by-step, building the structure of his character solidly as he went, but instead has rushed forward with panting haste, pretentiously. As a result, there is a great distance between Hitler at his best and Hitler at his worst, which means that when he is overcome at last by a greater force he will collapse suddenly and completely - and as an utter wreck.

2. Counter-Active Aggression, Revenge

That the will to power and the craving for superiority cannot account for the whole of Hitler's psychology is evidenced by his immeasurable hatred; hatred expressed in the absence of an adequate stimulus; an incessant need to find some object on which to vent his pent-up wrath. This can be traced back, with relative certainty, to experiences of insult, humiliation and wounded pride in childhood. The source of such insults, we have many reason to believe, was Hitler's fathe - a coarse, boastful man who ruled his wife (twenty-three years younger than himself) and his children with tyrannical severity and injustice.

2. (a) Explanation

The hypothesis is advanced, supported by much evidence, that as a boy Hitler was severely shocked (as it were, blinded) by witnessing sexual intercourse between his parents, and his reaction to this trauma was to swear revenge; to dream of himself as re-establishing the lost glory of his mother by overcoming and humiliating his father. The boy's relative weakness made this action impossible, and so the drive and passion of revenge was repressed and locked up within him under tension.

Only much later when a somewhat similar stimulus occurred - the subjugation and humiliation of his motherland (Hitler's term for Germany) in 1918 - was this energy of revenge released after a short period of shock and hysterical blindness. This would explain the fact that Hitler exhibited no energetic, ambitious drive of his own from the age of 13 years (when his father, the enemy, died) to the age of 29 years (when a new enemy, the conqueror of the motherland, appeared).

It also helps to account for Hitler's relentless devotion to the rehabilitation of Germany, a fact that is hard to explain in a man who is so extremely egocentric in other relations.

In *Mein Kampf* Hitler repeatedly speaks of Germany as a beloved woman.

(Note: In this connection it may be said that the evidence is in favor of Hitler's having experienced the common Oedipus Complex (love of mother, hate of father), but that in his case this pattern was repressed and submerged by another pattern: profound admiration, envy and emulation of his father's masculine power and contempt for his mother's feminine submissiveness and weakness. Thus both parents were ambivalent to him. His father was hated and respected, his mother was loved and depreciated. Hitler's conspicuous actions have all been in imitation of his father, not his mother.

Whether this genetical hypothesis is correct or not, it is certain that there is a vast reservoir of resentment and revenge in Hitler's make-up, which accounts for his cult brutality and his many acts of inexcusable destructiveness and cruelty. He is possessed by what amounts to a homicidal compulsion which has no vent in a "weak, piping time of peace," (unless he became an outright criminal), and therefore he has constantly pushed events toward war or scapegoating.

2. (b) Significance of Revenge

As a result of the fact that resentment is the

mainspring of Hitler's career, it is forever impossible to hope for any mercy or humane treatment from him. His revengefulness can be satisfied only by the extermination of his countless enemies.

3. Repression of Conscience, Compliance, Love

Unlike Goering and other associates, Hitler is no healthy, amoral brute. He is a hive of secret, neurotic compunctions and feminine sentiment-alities that have had to be stubbornly repressed ever since he embarked on his career of ruthless dominance and revenge (instigated by real or supposed insults).

Every new act of unusual cruelty, such as the purge of 1934, has been followed by a period of anxiety and depletion - agitated dejection and nightmares - which can be interpreted only as the unconscious operation of a bad conscience. Hitler wants nothing so much as to arrive at the state where he can commit crimes without guilt feelings; but despite his boasts of having transcended Good and Evil, this had not been possible. The suicidal trend in his personality is eloquent testimony of a repressed, self-condemning tendency.

In conjunction with the repression of conscience and the advance of hate there has been a repression of affection and sympathy as if "his spirit seemed to chide such weakness as unworthy of its pride," a reaction which sometimes occurs in childhood after an experience of unbearable disillusionment occasioned by the felt treachery of a beloved person. One may find "a vigilance of grief that would compel the soul to hate for having loved too well."

Hitler's affiliative tendencies have always been very weak.

He has never had any close personal friends. He is entirely incapable of normal human relationships. This is due, in part, to the cessation in early life of sexual development.

3. (a) Self-Vindicating Criminality

Paradoxical as it may seem, Hitler's repeated crimes are partly caused by conscience and the necessity of appeasing it. For having once set out on a life of crime, the man cannot turn back without reversing his entire ground for pride, and taking the humiliating path of self-abasement and atonement. The only method he has of subduing his mounting unconscious guilt is to commit another act of aggression, and so to prove, as it were, by the criterion of success, that his policy is favored by fortune and therefore justified and right. Failure is the only wrong.

3. (b) Significance of the Repression of Conscience by Successful Criminality

As soon as the time comes when repeated, offensive actions end in failure, Hitler will lose faith in himself and in his destiny and will become the helpless victim of his repressed conscience, with suicide or mental breakdown as the most likely outcome.

4. Projection of Criticize-able Elements of the Self

Hitler perceives in other people the traits or tendencies that are criticize-able in himself.

Thus, instead of being devoured by the vulture of his own condemning conscience or of his own disdain, he can attack what he apperceives as evil or contemptible in the external world, and so remain unconscious (most of the time) of his own guilt or his own inferiority. This Mechanism, whereby a man sees his own wicked impulses or weaknesses in others, is called projection. It is one way - the paranoid way- of maintaining self-esteem. The mechanism occurs so constantly in Hitler that it is possible to get a very good idea of the repudiated portions of his own personality by noticing what he condemns in others; treachery, lying, corruption, war-mongering, etc.

This mechanism would have had more disastrous consequences for his sanity if he had not gained some governance over it by consciously adopting, (as good political strategy) the practice of blaming his opponents.

5. Paranoid Symptoms

Hitler's dynamical pattern, as described,

corresponds closely to that of paranoid insanity. Indeed, he has exhibited, at one time or another, all of the classical symptoms of paranoid schizo-phrenia: hyper-sensitivity, panics of anxiety, irrational jealousy, delusions of persecution, delusions of omnipotence and messiah-ship.

How is it, then, that Hitler has escaped confinement as a dangerous psychopath? This interesting question will be considered later.

6. Reactions to Opposition and Frustration

Opposition is the stimulus which startles Hitler into life. In the face of it his powers are gathered and augmented. When opposition becomes stronger, resulting in severe frustration, his reaction has often been as follows:

1. Emotional outburst, tantrums of rage and accusatory indignation ending in tears and self-pity, succeeded by:

2. Periods of inertia, exhaustion, melancholy and indecisiveness (accompanied sometimes by hours of acute dejection and disquieting nightmares) leading to recuperation, and finally:

3. Confident and resolute decision to counter-attack with great force and ruthlessness. The entire cycle may run its course in twenty-four hours, or it may be weeks before the aggressive decision of the third stage is reached.

For years this pattern of reaction to frustration has met with success; each counter-attack has brought Hitler nearer to his goal. Since the turn of fortune on the Russian front, however, the number of frustrations have increased and Hitler's counter-attacks have failed, at times disastrously.

There is no structure for defense in Hitler's personality. He can only strike when inflated with confidence or collapse when confidence abandons him.

As time goes on, therefore, we can anticipate an increase in the intensity, frequency and duration of Hitler's periods of collapse, and a decrease in the confidence and power of his retaliations.

A point to be remembered about Hitler is that he started his career from scratch - a non-entity with nothing to lose - and he selected a fanatical path for himself which requires, as an ending, complete success (omnipotence) or utter failure (death).

No compromise is possible. Since it is not he personally who has to do the fighting, his collapses can occur in private at Berchtesgaden, where he can recuperate and then once again come back with some new and always more desperate plan to destroy the enemy.

There is a powerful compulsion in him to sacrifice himself and all of Germany to the revengeful annihilation of Western culture; to die, dragging all of Europe with him into the abyss. This, he would feel, was the last resource of an insulted and unendurable existence.

7. Need for Creation, Painting, Architecture, German State, Legend of Self

We surmise that Hitler's early enthusiasm for painting was due to the fact that:

1. This was the one exercise at which he excelled in school (and thus it offered a compensatory form of achievement):

2. That it provided an acceptable outlet for a destructive, soiling tendency repressed in infancy and:

3. That painting, and especially architecture later, also called for much constructiveness, which served to balance (operate as a reaction formation to, and atonement for) the primitive tendency to destroy.

Hitler has always enjoyed the painting of ruined temples (just as he has liked to contemplate the destruction of cities inhabited by his enemies); but he has likewise taken pleasure in painting immense castles (just as he has occupied himself designing buildings for the Third Reich).

A careful study of Hitler's writings and conduct has convinced us that he is not entirely devoted to destruction, as so many claim. In his nature there is a deep, valid strain of creativeness (lacking, to be sure, the necessary talent).

His creativity has been engaged in combining elements for an ideology, in organizing the National Socialist party, and in composing the allegory of his own life. He is the author and leading actor of a great drama.

Unlike other politicians, Hitler has conducted his life, at certain seasons, as a Romantic artist does, believing that it is the function of a nation's first statesman to furnish creative ideas, new policies and plans.

8. Repressed Need for Passivity and Abasement, Masochism

Hitler's long-concealed, secret heterosexual fantasy has been exposed by the systematic analysis and correlation of the three thousand odd metaphors he uses in Mein Kampf. The results of this study were later confirmed by the testimony of one who "claims to know." It is not necessary to describe its peculiar features here; suffice it to say that the sexual pattern has resulted from the fusion of:

1. A primitive, excretory soiling tendency and:

2. A passive, masochistic tendency; (hyper-trophy of the feminine component in his make-up). The second element, (masochism), derives much of its strength from an unconscious need for punishment, a tendency which may be expected in one who has assiduously repressed, out of swollen pride, the

submissive reactions; (compliance, cooperation, payment of debts, expression of gratitude, acknowledgment of errors, apology, confession, atonement), which are required of everybody who would adaptively participate in social life.

While Hitler consciously over-strives to assert his infinite superiority, nature instinctively corrects the balance by imposing an erotic pattern that calls for infinite self-abasement.

This erotic pattern, however, is not a strong force in Hitler's personality, nor does it comprise his entire libidinal investment. It alternates with other patterns; repressed (or as some claim, overt) homosexuality, for example.

What is important to recognize here is that the purpose of Hitler's prolonged counteractive efforts is not solely to rise above his humble origins, to overcome his weaknesses and ineptitudes, but rather to check and conquer, by means of a vigorous *ideal-ego reaction formation,* an underlying, positive craving for passivity and submission. There is no space here for the mass of evidence bearing on this point, but a few examples can be briefly listed:

1. The large feminine component in Hitler's physical constitution; also his feminine tastes and sensibilities:

2. His initial identification with his mother:

3. His exaggerated subservience, in the past, to

masterful superiors (army officers, Ludendorff, etc.):

4. Attraction to Roehm and other domineering homosexuals:

5. Hitler's nightmares which, as described by several informants, are very suggestive of homosexual panic:

6. Some of Hitler's interpretations of human nature, such as when he says that the people "want someone to frighten them and make them shudderingly submissive.

7. Hitler's repeated assertions that he intends, like Sulla, to abdicate power (after an orgy of conquest with full catharsis of his hate) and live quietly by himself painting and designing buildings; and finally:

8. Recurrent suicidal threats.

II. E.S. – Ideo-Centricity, Dedication to the Making of an Ideally Powerful Germany

No true German, friend or foe, has ever claimed that Hitler is not sincere in his devotion to the Prussian militarists' ideal for Germany. Thus we can say that he has been ideocentric (dedicated to an idea) for the last twenty years.

Because the idea consists of a plan for a society

from which the majority of his fellow countrymen will supposedly benefit, we can speak of him as socio-centric (**S**) also. But since this interest in his countrymen is clearly secondary to his personal ambition (fame, immortality), we put ego-centricity (**E**) first, and so write - **E. S.** Ideocentricity.

It is rare to find so much ideocentricity in a narcissistic personality; but only those who are incapable of such dedication are likely to doubt the reality of it in Hitler.

1. Insociation in Germany:

Since Hitler and a large body of the German people are mutually agreeable, we can speak of him as insociated - accepting and accepted. It is Hitler's intense affection for the-Reich (perhaps felt to this extent only by a nationalist born outside its boundaries) that has acted as a decisive factor in:

(1) His winning the support of the people and so satisfying his will to power.

(2) Giving him the feeling of vocation - the sense of mission.

(3) Providing moral justification (in his own mind) for many illegal acts, and;

(4) Keeping him relatively sane by bringing him into association with a group of like-minded men and so delivering him from the perils of psychological isolation.

Note. The supposition that, in Hitler's mind, Germany is identified with his mother, helps to explain the fervor of his dedication.

III. Sentiments

Most of Hitler's sentiments are well-known and have already been listed: his high valuation of Power, Glory, Dictatorship, Nationalism, Militarism and Brutality; and his low valuation of Weakness, Indecision, Tolerance, Compassion, Peace, Rational Debate, Democracy, Bolshevism, Materialism, Capitalism, the Jewish Race, Christianity.

A simplification would be that of regarding him as the advocate of the aggressive instinct (War, Power and Glory) vs the acquisitive instinct (Business, Peace and Prosperity).

Two questions deserve special consideration:

1. Why, when he was living as an outcast in Vienna, did Hitler not become a Communist? and

2. What is the explanation of Hitler's extreme Anti-Semitism?

1. Determinants of Hitler's Anti-Communism

1. (a) Hitler's father was an upwardly mobile individual Starting as a peasant, he worked his way into the lower middle class, establishing a boundary between himself and those below him. Both parents respected their social superiors. Thus Hitler instinctively retreated from too close association with the workmen of Vienna.

1. (b) Hitler was too frail for construction work - was unable to hold a job - and therefore had little opportunity to become associated with a Union.

1. (c) Having been an ardent nationalist since the age of 12, Hitler's line of cleavage - (conflict between nations) did not conform to the communists' line of cleavage - (conflict between classes).

1. (d) Hitler has always been an advocate of the hierarchical principle: government by the fittest - rigorously-trained and proven in action. The ideal of communism, on, the other hand, calls for a wide distribution of power among those untrained to rule.

1. (e) Hitler's sentiments have been with militarism from earliest youth. The materialism of Communism never appealed to him.

1. (f) Lacking sympathy for the underdog, the humanitarian aspect of communism did not attract him. Hitler has always been a bully.

2. Determinents of Hitler's Anti-Semitism

2. (a) The influence of wide-spread Anti-Semitic sentiments (represented especially by such men as Lueger and Feder), traditional in Germany.

2. (b) Hitler's personal frustrations required a scapegoat as focus for his repressed aggression. The Jew is the classic scapegoat because he does not fight back with fists and weapons.

.

2. (c) The Jew was an object upon whom Hitler could suitably project his own inferior self; (his sensitiveness, weakness, timidity, masochistic sexuality).

2. (d) After the Versailles Treaty, the German people also needed a scapegoat; Hitler offered them the Jewish race as an act of political strategy.

2. (e) Having assembled a veritable army of gangsters (Nazi troopers), and aroused their fighting spirit, it was necessary for Hitler to find some object upon whom these men could vent their brutish passions - to canalize anger away from himself.

2. (f) Jews, being non-militaristic, could only impede his program on conquest. In eliminating them he lost no sizeable support.

2. (g) Jews were associated with several of Hitler's pet antipathies: Business, Materialism, Democracy, Capitalism, Communism.

2. (h) Some Jews were very rich and Hitler needed an excuse for dispossessing them.

IV. Formal Structure, Hysteria, Schizophrenia

Hitler has a relatively weak character (ego structure); his great strength comes from an emotional complex which drives him periodically. Usually he cannot voluntarily force himself to stick to a routine of work; he must be compelled from inside - lifted on a wave of passion.. His Id (instinctual forces) and ego (voluntary control) are in league; his superego (conscience) is repressed:

1. Hysteria: Hitler has exhibited various forms of hysterical dissociation, most notably in the two symptoms which constituted his war neurosis in 1918, namely, blindness and sphonia (mutism). He experiences periods of marked abstraction, violent emotional outbursts, visions or hallucinatory clarity. In speaking before crowds he is virtually possessed. He clearly belongs to the sensational company of history-making hysterias, combining, as he does, some of the attributes of the primitive shaman; the religious visionary and the crack-brained dema-gogue - consumate actors, one and all.

It is important to note, however, that Hitler has a large measure of control over his complexes. He uses an emotional outburst to get his own way, turning it on or off as the occasion requires. As Erikson says, he; "*knows how to exploit his hysteria...On the stage of German history, Hitler senses to what extent it is safe and expedient to let his own personality represent, with hysterical abandon, what lives in every German listener and reader.*"

2. Schizophrenia: Psychiatrists are not unfamiliar with borderline states lying between hysteria and schizophrenia. In some cases the former develops into the latter (a serious variety of insanity).

Since Hitler, as noted above, has exhibited all the symptoms of paranoid schizophrenia, the possibility of a complete mental breakdown is not remote.

Here, again, however, it should be observed that paranoid dynamics can be used very effectively in rousing and focusing the forces of a minority party or a defeated nation. The strategy consists chiefly in; **(i)** painting vivid and exaggerated word-pictures of the crimes and treacherous evil purposes of your powerful opponents (delusions of persecution); **(ii)** persuading your own group of its innate superiority and glorious destiny (delusions of grandeur); **(iii)** subduing conscience by asserting that your common end justifies the means that your opponents have used the most dastardly means in the past and; **(iv)** blaming your enemies for every frustration, every disaster that occurs. In consciously employing these tactics Hitler has exploited his own paranoid trends and retained some governance over them.

Thus, the answer to the question; how has Hitler escaped veritable insanity? might be this; **(i)** he has gained a large measure of control over his hysterical and paranoid trends by using them consciously and successfully in the achievement of his aims; **(ii)** he has identified himself with and dedicated himself to a sociocentric purpose (the creation of an ideal Germany) which has served to diminish the pains and perils of an isolated egocentrism and; **(iii)** he has been supremely successful in imposing his visions and delusions (conforming, as they did, with existent trends) upon the German people, and so convincing them of his unparalleled superiority. Thus his unreal world has become real – his insanity is sanity.

V. 1. Abilities and .Effective Traits

Hitler's success has depended, to a large extent, upon his own peculiar abilities and traits.

1. (a) The ability to express with passion, the deepest needs and longings of the people.

1. (b) The ability to appeal to the most primitive, as well as to the most ideal tendencies in men.

1. (c) The ability to simplify complex problems and arrive at the quickest solution.

1. (d) The ability to use metaphor and draw on traditional imagery and myth in speaking and writing.

1. (e) The ability to evoke the sympathy and protectiveness of his people - The leader's welfare becomes a matter of concern to them.

1. (f) Complete dedication to his mission - abundant self-confidence and stubborn adherence to a few principles.

1. (g) Mastery of the art of political organization.

1. (h) Tactical genius; precise timing.

1. (i) Mastery of the art of propaganda.

2. Principles of Political Action.

Among the guiding principles of Hitler's political philosophy, the following are worth listing:

2 (a) Success depends on winning the support of the masses.

2. (b) The leader of a new movement must appeal to youth.

2. (c) The masses need a sustaining ideology: it is the function of the leader to provide one.

2. (d) People do not act if their emotions are not roused.

2. (e) Artistry and drama are necessary to the total effect of political rallies and meetings.

2. (f) The leading statesman must be a creator of ideas and plans.

2. (g) Success justifies any means.

2. (h) A new movement cannot triumph without the effective use of terroristic methods.

B. Predictions of Hitler's Behavior

Whatever else happens it can be confidently predicted that Hitler's neurotic spells will increase in frequency and duration and his effectiveness as a leader will diminish: responsibility will fall, to a greater or lesser extent, on other shoulders. Indeed, there is some evidence that his mental powers have been deteriorating since last November, 1942. Only once or twice has he appeared before his people to enlighten or encourage them. Aside from the increase in neurotic symptoms, the following things might happen:

1. Hitler may be forcefully seized by the Military Command or by some revolutionary faction in Germany and be immured in some prison fortress.

This event is hard to envisage in view of what we know of the widespread reverence for the man and the protection that is afforded him. But if this were to occur, the myth of the invincible hero would end rather ignominiously, and Hitler should eventually be delivered into our hands. The General Staff will no doubt become the rulers of Germany if Hitler's mental condition deteriorates much further (option #5).

2. Hitler may be shot by some German. The man has feared this eventuality for many years and today he is protected as never before. Germans are not inclined to shoot their leaders. This is possible but not very likely.

3. Hitler may arrange to have himself shot by a German, perhaps by a Jew. This would complete the myth of the hero - death at the hand of some trusted follower - Siegfried Stabbed in the back by Hagen, Caesar by Brutus, Christ betrayed by Judas. It might increase the fanaticism of the soldiers for a while and create a legend in conformity with the ancient pattern. If Hitler could arrange to have a Jew - some paranoid like himself - kill him, then he could die in the belief that his fellow countrymen would rise in their wrath and massacre every remaining Jew in Germany. Thus he might try to indulge his insatiable revengefulness for the last time.

4. Hitler may get himself killed leading his elite troops in battle. Thus he would live on as a hero in the hearts of his countrymen. It is not unlikely that he will choose this course, which would be very undesirable from our point of view, first because his death would serve as an example to all his followers to fight with fanatical, death-defying energy to the bitter end; and second, because it would insure Hitler's immortality - the Siegfried who led the Aryan hosts against Bolshevism and the Slav. This is one of Hitler's favorite poses.

5. Hitler may go insane. The man has been on the verge of paranoid schizophrenia for years and with the mounting load of frustration and failure he may yield his will to the turbulent forces of the unconscious. This would not be undesirable from our standpoint because, even if the fact were hidden from the people, morale would rapidly deteriorate as rumors spread, and the legend of the hero would be severely damaged by the outcome. If Hitler became insane, he would eventually fall into the hands of the Allied Nations.

6. Hitler may commit suicide. Hitler has often vowed that he would commit suicide if his plans miscarried, but if he chooses this course he will do it at the last moment and in the most dramatic manner possible. He will retreat, let us say, to the impregnable little refuge that was built for him on the top of the mountain behind the Berghof (Berchtesgaden). There alone he will wait until troops come to take him prisoner. As a grand climax he will either **(i)** blow up the mountain and end himself with dynamite; or **(ii)** make a funeral pyre of his dwelling and throw himself on it (a fitting gotterdammerung);or **(iii)** kill himself with a silver bullet (Emperor Christophe); or **(iv)** throw himself off the parapet. This outcome, undesirable for us is not at all unlikely.

7. Hitler may die of natural causes.

8. Hitler may seek refuge in a neutral country This is not likely, but one of his associates might drug him and take him to Switzerland in a plane and then persuade him that he should stay there to write his long-planned Bible for the German folk. Since the Hero's desertion of his people would seriously damage the legend, this outcome would be more desirable than some of the other possibilities.

9. Hitler may fall into the hands of the United Nations. This is perhaps the least likely, but the most desirable, outcome.

In making these predictions we have been swayed most by the supposition that Hitler's chief concern is the immortality of his legend and consequently he will endeavor to plan his own end according to the most heroic, tragic and dramatic pattern.

Options #5 (insanity to some extent) and #6 (dramatic suicide), or #4 (death at the front), strike us as most probable today.

Propaganda measures should, if possible, be devised to prevent #4 and #6.

C. Suggestions for the treatment of Hitler.

1. After the defeat of Germany, if Hitler is taken into custody by the United Nations, any one of the conventional punishments - a trial followed by execution, by life imprisonment or by exile - will provide a tragic ending for the drama of Hitler's sensational career, and thus contribute the element that is necessary to the resurrection and perpetuation of the Hitler legend. What can the Allies do that will spell the tragedy and thus kill the legend? As an answer to this question, the following plan is suggested,. It should work if properly executed.

1. (a) Bring the Nazi leaders to trial; Condemn the

chief culprits to death, but proclaim Hitler mentally unbalanced.

1. (b) Commit Hitler to an insane asylum (such as St. Elisabeth's, Washington, D.C.) and house him in a comfortable dwelling specially built for his occupancy. Let the world know that he is being well treated..

1. (c) Appoint a committee of psychiatrists and psychologists to examine him and test his faculties at regular intervals. Unbeknownst to him, have sound films taken of his behavior. They will show his fits and tirades and condemnations to everyone in the world, including the Germen people.

1. (d) Exhibit regularly to the public of the entire world selected segments of these sound-reels, so that it can be seen how unbalanced he is; how mediocre his performance on the customary tests. If taken in a routine, scientific and undramatic manner, the pictures will become quite tiresome after a while and the people will get bored with Hitler in a year or so. (Trust in science to take the drama out of anything.)

1. (e) Hitler's case should be presented to the world as a lesson: "*This is what happens to crack-brained fanatics who try to dominate the world.*"

As such it could serve as a powerful deterrent to others with fantasies of world domination.

1. (f) A thorough study of Hitler's personality

would be of considerable importance to psychiatry, and the publication of a carefully documented book on the subject (published in popular form) would not only act as a deterrent to future would-be Hitlers, but would be a significant contribution to science.

2. Between Now and the Cessation of Hostilities.

The aim should be either **(i)** to accelerate Hitler's mental deterioration, to drive him insane; or **(ii)** to prevent him from insuring the perpetuation of his legend by ending his life dramatically and tragically.

There are various psychological techniques available for accelerating Hitler's nervous break-down, but they will not be considered here None could be so certainly effective as repeated military setbacks.

We shall limit ourselves to a few measures which might serve to; **(a)** deter Hitler from arranging a hero's or a martyr's death for himself, and; **(b)** to make him believe that the immortality of his legend will not suffer if he falls into the hands of the United Nations. **(c)** Flood Germany with communications - leaflets, short-wave, long-wave, official speeches, underground transmission from Sweden, Switzerland and Turkey - telling the people that Hitler cannot be trusted; that he is planning (quoting Hess, Strasser, Hanfstaerigel, Rauschning and other Nazis in England and America) to leave them treacherously to their fate by getting himself killed. This will be a sly trick of his to insure his own prestige and future fame. He does not care for the German people; he cares only for his own glory. He is no better than a sea-captain who quits his ship, leaving his crew to drown. Drop vivid cartoons of Hitler rushing ludicrously forward to his death on the Russian front (out of a guilty conscience over the noble Germans he has condemned to die there for his glory); also, cartoons of his arranging to have himself shot and others of his committing suicide. Interpret this as the easy way out, a cowardly betrayal of his people, the act of a bad conscience, the quintessence of vanity. Warn the people against him, the false prophet - the Judas Iscariot of the German Revolution, etc., etc . If hundreds of these leaflets, pamphlets and streamers are dropped over Berchtesgaden, the chances are that some of them will fall in places where Hitler himself is likely to come on them. He is very susceptible to ridicule; and if the cartoons are clever enough to make suicide seem cowardly, grotesque or ridiculous, it may be enough to deter him. Prediction will spoil the startling effect.

2. (b) Flood Germany with another series of communications in which the people are told that the Nazi leaders who led them into this disastrous war are going to be executed - all except Hitler who will be exiled to Saint Helena where he can brood over his sins for the rest or his life. Write as if we thought that this was the most terrible of all punishments; but actually this idea should appeal to Hitler, who greatly admires Napoleon and knows that the Napoleonic legend was fostered by the man's last years at Saint Helena. This treatment would be better than any he could now be hoping to receive from his enemies. It might positively attract him. He would imagine himself painting landscapes, writing his new Bible, and making plans for an even greater German revolution to be carried out in his name thirty years hence.

By the repeated and not too obvious use of these two messages, Hitler would be faced by a conflict between; **(1)** a self-annihilation which might be interpreted as a cowardly betrayal, and; **(2)** a peaceful old age at Saint Helena. He might choose the latter and so allow himself to be taken by the Allies. Only later Would he discover that there was to be no Saint Helena for him. This trick of ours is justified by the necessity of preventing the resurrection of the memory of Hitler as a superman to rouse future generations of criminals and revolutionaries.

D. Suggestions for the Treatment of the German People.

I. Hastening the Breakdown of Germany's Faith in Hitler.

The German people have put their whole trust in Hitler. He is their man, as no military commander representing a special class could be their man. Having taken the entire responsibility for the conduct of affairs, he has become their conscience and so relieved them temporarily of guilt. The pride, system and security of each individual German is thus based on Hitler's genius and success. The bulk of the people will not easily be persuaded of his incompetence and falseness. They will cling as long as possible to the illusion of his omniscience because without this they have nothing. When it comes, the disenchantment will be sudden and catastrophic to German morale generally.

The Allies can rely on the march of physical events to bring about the eventual disenchantment of the German peoples, but since events will march faster and the war will end sooner if this disenchantment can be hastened by other means, the Allies should not overlook the power of words to change sentiments and attitudes. The following suggestions may prove of some value:

1. (a) Technique of communication.

One effective method would be that of printing leaflets containing the names, ranks and regiments of German soldiers recently taken prisoner. The Gestapo could hardly succeed in preventing anxious parents from picking up these leaflets to obtain the latest news of their sons at the front. Communications of this sort might start somewhat as follows: *NEWS FROM THE FRONT*; Among the 20,000 German soldiers who surrendered to the World Army in Sicily, the following were happy at the prospect of going to America, the land of free speech and free action: Corp. Hans Schmidt, Capt. Heinrich-Wittels, etc. etc. "Why are you laughing?" they were asked. "Because," they answered, "we are going to the United States; whereas you are going to the land of the False Prophet and the Gestapo!" etc., etc.

We suggest that *NEWS FROM THE FRONT* be distributed at regular weekly intervals like a newspaper, in order that the Germans will learn to expect it and look forward to it since it will contain news that they cannot obtain in any other way. Mixed in with the lists of German prisoners could be printed the messages that, "we to impart to the people:

1. (b) (Name for Hitler). In the minds of many Germans, the word "Hitler" is still surrounded by a layer of reverential feelings which protect his image from attack. Therefore, it would be better not to refer to him (except occasionally) by name. Much more subtly effective would be the use of another term, such as False Prophet or False Messiah. Later, more derogatory terms - the Amateur Strategist, Corporal Satan, World Criminal No. 1 - might be effective.

1. (c) Substitution of a Higher Symbol.

The German character-structure is marked by a strong need to worship, obey and sacrifice. When this can be focused on some entity - God, the Absolute, the German State, the Fuhrer – they are happy and healthy. Consequently, it will be easier to break their present allegiance to Hitler if a satisfactory substitute is presented. Germans will not readily accept a value that is identified in their minds with the special preferences of an enemy-nation (Democracy, etc.) It must be something higher; something, supra-national that will excite the respect of all peoples.

There is a great need now, rather than later, for some form of World Federation. But lacking this, the Allies, in their message to Germany, should use terms that suggest its spirit. Against Hitler, the False Prophet, the propagandists should speak of the World Conscience (the name of God cannot be used without hypocrisy), and should speak of the forces of Russia, Great Britain, France and the Americas as the World Army; (N.B. Suggestion for one leaflet: Question: Who has seduced the German people from their true path? Who has turned their hearts against the Conscience of the World? Who is responsible this time for Germany's encirclement by the World Army?) To be, effective the terms "World Conscience" and World Army" should be repeated frequently. "World Police Force might also be used.

1. (d) A collection should be made of passages from the first unexpurgated edition of *Mein Kampf*, demonstrating Hitler's cynical contempt of the Masses. Each NEWS FROM THE FRONT should end with one of these quotations:

1. (e) Identification of Hitler with Mussolini – Mussolini provided the model for the development of the Nazi Party and Hitler publicly expressed his admiration for the Italian leader. (His words on this point should be reprinted.) Mussolini's fall will do

much to undermine German morale, and no opportunity should be missed to stress the connection between Hitlers' destiny and Mussolini's defeat - the Decline and Fall of the Unholy Alliance.

1. (f) The Conception of Destiny. Germans believe in predestination (the wave of the future), and all communications addressed to them should be written as if the defeat of the False Prophet was a foregone conclusion. Some messages should come from the "Voice of History."

1. (g) Taking Advantage of Hitlers' Waning Powers. Hitler's precise status and role in German Politics at this moment is not definitely known; but the decreasing frequency of his appearances is probably due to a growing inability to fulfill his former function. His mental state is evidently deteriorating. This should be assumed in talking to the German people. For example: "Now that Mussolini has collapsed and Hitler is in the hands of mental specialists, what has become of the Spirit of Fascism?" or, "Do still believe that a man whose sanity has been completely undermined, by Guilt can lead the German. people to victory against the World?"

1. (h) Germany's One Remaining Ally, Japan. The Nazi regime should be constantly coupled with Japan in an ironic or satirical manner. For example; "The Nazis and their blood brothers, the Japanese, have both demonstrated their willingness to die for Satan. This summer one million of them have thrown away their lives in a futile attempt to destroy civilization. Who is responsible for this ignoble league of Germany and Japan against the Conscience of the World? A fact to be explained: Germans are dying every day fighting with the Japanese against: German-Americans. Why is that? Who is responsible?"

1. (i) Munich Student Manifesto. In planning messages to Germany, hints for one line of propaganda can be obtained from the revolutionary manifesto distributed last year by students at the University of Munich.

2. Peace Terms – Trials of War Criminals

2. (a) Psychologically, it is important that Hitler, or the leader of the Nazi Party, be the one to surrender and sign the peace treaty. The Allies should insist on this, should drag the gangsters without ceremony from their hiding places and force them to sign. (A little trickery at this point would be justified.) The terms should be severe, at first. Later, when a more representative government has been established, the terms can be made more lenient: Thus, in the future, dictators will be recalled in the humiliation of unconditional surrender, whereas the democratic government will get the credit of securing milder terms.

2. (b) A World Court, at least one member of which is a Swiss and one a Swede, should immediately publish list of their criminals, as complete as possible, and neutral Countries should be officially

warned that no man on this list must be given sanctuary. The Allies should be prepared to invade any country that harbors world criminals.

2. (c) The trial of the war criminals should be carried out with the utmost dispatch; it must not be allowed to drag on for months, as this would give the Germans a convincing impression of our moral weakness and incompetence, and postpone their regeneration. In connection with the trial, a short, readable book should be published in German explaining the nature of international law (the brotherhood of' nations), and exposing the crimes committed by the Fascists in A.B.C. language. A pamphlet comparing the terms of the Versailles Treaty with Germany's method of dealing with conquered countries should be given wide circulation.

3. Treatment of the German People after the Cessation of Hostilities.

It is assumed that Germany will be invaded and occupied by Allied forces, that simultaneously there will be uprisings of slave labor and civilians in occupied territories, and that much German blood will be spilled. This is as it should be a - fitting Nemesis. The Allied troops will march in and eventually restore order. This function of restoring order will make their presence more acceptable to the Germans. It can be predicted that we will find the German people profoundly humiliated, resentful, disenchanted, dejected, morose - despairing of the future. Accustomed to obeying an arbitrary, external authority, they will have no dependable inner guides to control behavior. There will be a wave of crime and suicide. Apathy will be widespread. Having passed through a period of intense unanimity and cooperation, Germany as a social system will fall apart, leaving each man to suffer pain and mortification in private.

Disorganization and confusion will be general, creating a breeding ground for cults of extreme individualism. A considerable part of the population will be weighed down by a heavy sense of guilt, which should lead to a revival of religion.. The soil will be laid for a spiritual regeneration, and perhaps the Germans, not we ,will inherit the future.

It is assumed that the Allies will demilitarize Germany and will insist on efficient guarantees against future conspiracies; will take steps to liquidate the Junker Class; will prevent rearmament and the misuse of raw materials. As Dr. Foerster has said: a soft peace for Germany will be a very hard peace for the German people, delivering them to the Prussian caste who led them astray.

Nothing permanent, however, can he achieved by such measures alone. What is required is a profound abandonment of the idea; **(i)** that they are innately superior; **(ii)** that they are destined to govern the earth; **(iii)** that there is no human law or authority higher than the good of the German State; **(iv)** that power is to be admired above everything, and; **(v)** that Might makes Right.

In treating the Germans psychologically, we must realize that we are dealing with a nation suffering from paranoid trends: delusions of grandeur, delusions of persecution; profound hatred of strong opponents and contempt for weak opponents; arrogance, suspiciousness and envy, all of which has been built up as a reaction to an age-old inferiority complex and a desire to be appreciated.

Possibly, the first four steps in the treatment of a single, paranoid personality can he adapted to the conversion of Germany. In attempting this, we must not forget that the source of their psychic sickness is wounded pride.

3. (a) First Step: the physician must gain the respect of the patient:

(i) The individual paranoid. Paranoids cannot be treated successfully if they are not impressed (consciously or unconsciously) by the ability, knowledge, wisdom, (or perhaps the mere magnetic force) of the physician. Special efforts must sometimes be made to achieve this end since paranoids, being full of scorn, are not easy to impress.

(ii) The regiments that occupy Germany should be the finest that the United Nations can assemble - regiments with a history of victories - composed of well-disciplined soldiers commanded by the best generals. Rowdiness and drunkenness should not be permitted. The Germans should be compelled to admit; "These are splendid men, not the weak degenerates (democratic soldiers) or barbarians

(Russian soldiers) that we were led to expect. The Germans admire orderliness, precision, efficiency.

3. (b) Second Step: The potential worth of the patient should be fully acknowledged. **(i)** Individual, paranoid: The indwelling, burning hunger of the paranoid is for recognition, power and glory - praise from those whom he respects. This hunger should be appeased as soon as possible so that the paranoid thinks to himself; "The great man appreciates me. Together we can face the worlds." It is as if he thought; "He is God the father and I am his chosen son."

(ii) Germany - Germany's country-side; its music, historic culture and monuments of beauty should be appreciated and praised. The army of occupation should manifest intense interest in the culture of Old Germany, and show complete indifference to all recent developments. The troops should be instructed and coached by lectures and guide-books covering the district they will occupy. they should be told that the war is not be won until the heart of the German people has been won.

Germans of the old school should be hired to teach the German language; to guide the soldiers on tours of the country and of museums; to teach native arts and skills. Concerts should be arranged, omitting pieces that have been specially favored by the Nazis. Editions of books burned by the Nazis should be published and put on sale immediately. All this will serve a double purpose. It will provide education for our troops and occupy their time, thus helping to maintain morale. Also, the submerged inferiority feelings and resentments of the Germans will be alleviated.

3. (c) Third Step. Insight should be tactfully provided, a little at a time.

(i) Individual Paranoid. Very gradually, step by step, the patient is enlightened as to his own paranoid mechanisms. Pride in being un-criticizable and always in the right must be gradually replaced by pride in being able to rise above his own mechanism and criticize himself; pride in being strong enough to admit some weaknesses and errors. He should be made to understand that he has been victimized by unconscious forces which gained control over his proper self. During the course of these talks, the physician should freely confess his own weaknesses and errors, the patient being treated as an equal.

(ii) Germany. The last ten years of German history should be interpreted as a violent, infectious fever; a possession of the spirit which took hold of the people as soon as they gave ear to the false prophets of Fascism.

A series of articles, editorials, essays and short books should be written now by Germans in this country, (Thomas Mann, Reinhold Niebuhr, Foerster and others), aided possibly by suggestions from psychiatrists, to be published in German newspapers and distributed soon after the occupation. They should be therapeutic essays, essentially – perhaps signed by a nom-de-plume as if written by a minister, physician or writer in Germany.

Not too much should be said in any one paper; but in time, the lies, delusions, treacheries and crimes of the Nazi party should be reviewed objectively in historical sequence. The Gorman people should be made to understand that the world regards them as unwitting and unhappy victims of instinctual forces. The Allies should be magnanimous enough to admit their own errors and misdeeds.

3. (d) Fourth Step; The patient should be insociated in a group.

(i) Individual paranoid. Having attained a measure of satisfaction by winning the respect and friendship of his physician and then having gained some insight and control, the patient is ready for group therapy. Later, he can be persuaded to join outside groups. Gradually, he must learn to take his place and cooperate on an equal basis with others. The group he joins should have a goal.

(ii) Germany; If Germany is to be converted, it is of the utmost importance that some strong and efficient super-government be established as soon as possible, providing a new world conscience that her people can respect. As said above, Germans must have something to look up to - a God, a Fuehrer, an Absolute, a national ideal. It cannot be a rival nation, or a temporary alliance of nations. It must be a body, a strong body with a police force which stands above any single state. A supra-national symbol would eventually attract the deference that is now focused upon Hitler. Lacking such a symbol, many Germans will certainly fall into a state of profound disillusionment and despair. At the proper time, Germany should be insociated as an equal in whatever league or federation of nations has been established.

From here on, the therapy of a single paranoid personality fails as an analogy, principally because the German people will not be in the position of a patient who comes willingly to the physician's office. The Nazis will be in no mood to be educated by their enemies. Furthermore, it would be very presumptuous of us to try it. The most that the Allies could do would be to close all schools and universities until new, anti-fascist teachers and faculties had been recruited. The greatest problem will be in dealing whole generation of brutalized and hardened young Nazis. (Perhaps exhibition games of soccer, football, lacrosse and baseball between American and English regiments would serve to introduce ideas of fair play and sports-manship; but much else must be done by German educators).

For the conversion of Germany, the most effective agency will be some form of world federation. Without this, the Allied victory will have no permanently important consequences.

SECTION II

Hitler the Man – Notes for a Case History

by W. H. D. Vernon
Harvard University

The purpose of this paper is to bring together in
brief form what is known about Adolf Hitler as a
man. For if Allied strategists could peer "inside
Hitler" and adapt their Strategy to what they find
there, it is likely that the winning of the war would
be speeded. It must be admitted, to begin with, that
the intricacies of so complex a personality would
be difficult enough to unravel were the subject
present and cooperating in the task. But there are
two further difficulties to be faced. One must
attempt both to select out of the great mass of
material which has been written about Hitler that
which appears to be objective reporting and then
further to reconstruct his personality on the basis of
this very inadequate psychological data. We have,
of course, as primary source material, Hitler's own
writings and speeches and these tell us a good deal.
Though we must admit, therefore, at its beginning,
that the nature of our analysis is very tentative and
that in many instances only imperfect proof can be
given for the inferences which are drawn, it is no
more tentative than the psychological pen pictures
which the Nazis themselves have found so useful.
(3)

HITLER'S ORIGINS AND EARLY LIFE

In any case study one most begin by asking who the subject is, whence he came, who were his forbears. Heiden (8) presents the most reliable genealogy available. Here we note only certain important points.

Hitler's father, Alois, was born the illegitimate son of Maria Anna Schicklgruber in 1837 in the village of Spital. He was supposed to be the son of Johann Georg Hiedler However, to his fortieth year, (1) Alois bore the name of his mother Schicklgruber. Only then, when Georg Hiedler was (if still alive) (2) eighty-five years of age, and thirty-five years after the death of his mother, did he take the name of Hitler, the maiden name of his mother-in-law. As Heiden says; "In the life history of Adolf Hitler no mention is ever made of: the grandparents on his father's side.

1. January 6, 1877
2. There seems to be no record of his death.

The details invariably refer only to his mother's relations. There are many things to suggest that Adolph Hitler's grandfather was not Johann Georg Hiedler, but an unknown man. (6, 8) The ancestors on both sides of the family were peasant people of the district of Waldviertel, highly illiterate and very inbred. (5, 8)

Alois Hitler, at first a cobbler, had, by the age of forty, achieved the position of an Austrian customs official. The education for this position was the contribution of his first wife, Anna Glasl, who, fifteen years his senior, died in 1883. His second wife, whom he married six weeks later, died in a year, and three months later, on January 7, 1885, (5) he married Klara Polzl, a distant cousin.

In appearance, Heiden has compared Alois to Hindenburg. (6) Gunther (5) describes his picture as showing a big, round, hairless skull; small, sharp, wicked eyes; big bicycle-handle mousta-chios, and a heavy chin. He was a harsh, stern, ambitious, and punctilious man. (5; 8)

Alois' wife, Klara, is described (5) as being a tall, nervous young woman, not as strong as most peasant stock, who ran off to Vienna as a girl to return in ten years, (a daring escapade for one in her social status).

Her doctor (1) describes her in her early forties as tall with brownish hair neatly-plaited, a long oval face and beautifully expressive grey blue eyes. A simple, modest, kindly woman.

Adolf Hitler, born in 1889, as far as can be ascertained (3), was Alois' fifth child - the third of his own mother but the first to live more than two Tears. (4) This, it would seem, was a large factor in channeling the great affection for Adolf which all the evidence seems to show she bore him. In return, Adolf, who feared and opposed his father, (as he himself admits), gave all his affection to his mother, and when she died of cancer in 1908, he was prostrated with grief. **(8, 9, 1)**

.

Adolf as a boy and youth was somewhat tall, sallow and old for his age with large, melancholy, thoughtful eyes. He was neither robust nor sickly, and with but the usual infrequent ailments of a cold or sore throat. That he had lung trouble is a common and natural belief **(9)**, but his doctor says "no." **(1)**

3. Heiden points out that the uncertain details of Hitler's family have had to be collected from stray publications; that Hitler is reticent to the point of arousing suspicion about his life story. (8)

4. Alois' children were Alois, 1882, (son by first wife), Angela, 1883, (daughter by second wife); Gustave, 1885-87; a daughter, 1886-88; Adolf, 1889; Edmund, 1894-1900; Paula, 1895 or '96, (children by third wife).

His recreations were such as were free – walks in the mountains, swimming in the Denube - and . reading Fenimore Cooper and Karl May **(5)**; a quiet, well-mannered youth who lived with himself. **(6)**

About Adolf's early education we know little except what he himself tells us; that he early wanted to be an artist; that this outraged his father, who sternly determined to make a good civil servant out of him; that there was perpetual struggle be-tween the two, with his mother siding with Adolf and finally sending him off to Vienna to complete his art education when his father died.

Except for history and geography, which caught his imagination, he neglected his studies to find in Vienna, when he failed his art examinations, that his lack of formal education was a barrier to entering the architectural school.

At the age of nineteen, when his mother died, he went to Vienna to spend there three lonely and miserable years, living in "flop-houses," (7) eking out a living by begging, shoveling snow, peddling his own postcards, working as a hod.-carrier or casual laborer of any sort. Here is ideas began to crystalize – his anti-Semitism and anti-Slavism – his ideas of all sorts.

5. A German author of Indian stories.
6. This in contrast to Hitler's own account of himself as a bit of a young tough. (9)

In 1912 he went to Munich and lived there as a water-color artist, picture postcard painter and technical draftsman and occasional house-painter. Hitler managed to earn some sort of a living. (8, 25)

In 1914 he enlisted in the army with great enthusiasm, performed his duties with distinction and bravery, (7) was wounded, sent home to re-cover, and in March, 1917, went back to the front. He was aloof from comrades, serious in his duty, and very lonely. Through all the war he received no letter or parcel. (8)

The war, over and with no home to go to, Hitler, in 1919, was appointed an espionage agent of the insurgent Reichswehr which had just put down the

Soviet Republic; in Yunich. Shortly thereafter he came in contact with Anton Drexler, and what was to later become the Nazi party had its beginning. Further than this it is not necessary to follow Hitler's political history. It is too well-known, and the basic structure of his personality was already formed. Later years have only brought to fruition latent tendencies and laid the final product open for the world to wonder at. We must now turn to a closer examination of this structure.

7. **Military awards were: Regimental Diploma for Conspicuous Bravery, Military Cross for Distinguished Service Third Class, The Black Wounded Badge, and The Iron Cross First Class (8)**

HITLER'S PERSONAL APPEARANCE AND MANNER

Portraits or moving pictures of Hitler are common enough, yet it is well to draw attention to various aspects of his physique. To most non-Nazis, Hitler has no particular attraction. He resembles a second rate waiter. He is a smallish man, slightly under average height. His forehead is slightly receding and his nose somewhat incongruous with the rest of his face. The latter is somewhat soft, his lips thin and the whole face expressionless. The eyes are a neutral grey which tend to take on the color of their momentary surroundings. (8) The look tends to be staring or dead and lacking in sparkle. There is an essentially feminine quality about his person which is portrayed particularly in his strikingly well-shaped and expressive hands. (2; 8; 13; et al:)

8. This fact has caused an amazing number of different descriptions of his actual eye color.

Hitler's manner is essentially awkward, and all his movements jerky except perhaps the gestures of his hands. He appears shy and ill at ease in company and seems seldom capable of carrying on conversation.

Usually he declaims while his associates listen. He often seems listless and moody. This is in marked contrast to the dramatic energy of his speeches and his skillful play upon the emotions of his vast audiences, every changing mood of which he appears to perceive and to turn to his own purposes.

At times he is conciliatory, at other times he may burst into violent temper tantrums if his whims are checked in any way. (16)

ATTITUDES, TRAITS AND NEEDS CHARACTERISTIC OF HITLER

Attitudes Towards Nature, Fate, Religion

First last words are often significant. Mein Kampf begins with a sentiment of gratitude to Fate, and almost its last paragraph appeals for vindication to the Goddess of History. However, all through the book there are references to Eternal Nature, Providence and Destiny; "Therefore, I believe today I am acting in the sense of the Almighty creator: by warding off the Jews I am fighting for the Lord's work." (9, 84) This feeling of being directed by. great forces outside one – of doing the Lord's work - is the essence of feeling of the religious mystic. No matter how pagan Hitler's ethical and social ideas may be, they have a quality comparable to religious experience. Moreover, all through his acts and words, both spoken and written, is this extreme exaggeration of his own self-importance -- he truly feels his divine mission, (16) even to the point of foreseeing a martyr's death. (16)

As far as authorized religion is concerned, Hitler recognized both its strength and weaknesses (9, 12) and adopted freely whatever he found serviceable for his own ends. That he strikes down Protestant and Catholic alike is due merely to the conviction that these religions are but old husks and must give way to the new. (9)

Toward conscience his attitude is a dual one. On the one hand he repudiates it as an ethical guide, heaping contempt on it as a Jewish invention, a blemish like circumcision. (16) He scorns as fools those who obey it. (1) But in matters of action he waits upon his inner voice;'"Unless I have the inner incorruptible conviction, *this is the solution*, I do nothing,..I will not act,..I will wait, no matter what happens. But if the voice speaks, then I know the time has come to act. (19, 181)

Like Socrates, he listens to his Daimon.

Hitler's Attitude Towards Power and His Need for Aggression.

To the German people, and to the world at large, Hitler appears as a man of tremendous strength of will, determination and power. Yet, those who are or have been close to him (e.g., 16) know that he is conscious of being powerful, and impresses others as such, only at certain times. When he is declaiming to a great throng or when he is on one of his solitary walks through the mountains, then Hitler is conscious of his destiny as one of the great and powerful of the ages. But in between these periods he feels humiliated and weak. At such times he is irritated and unable to do or decide anything. It is these feelings of his own weakness that no doubt have determined, to a great extent, his ideas on the education of youth. All weakness must be knocked out of the new German youth; they must be Indifferent to pain; have no fear of death; must learn the art of self-command; for only in this way can they become creative God-men (10). Hitler's feelings of weakness and power probably also determine his attitudes towards peoples and nations. For those who are weak, or for some reason do not display power, he has only contempt. (9)

9. **"My great political opportunity lies in my deliberate use of power at a time when there are still illusions abroad as to the forces that mold history." (16, 271).**

For those who are strong he has feelings of respect, fear, submissiveness (4, 9, 16). For the Britain of the great war period he had great respect (9), but only contempt for the powerless Indian revolutionaries who tried to oppose British imperial power (9).**(10)**

For the masses over whom he has sway, he feels only contempt. He compares them to a woman who prefers to submit to the will of someone stronger (9). He harangues the crowd at night when they are tired and less resistant to the will of another (9). He uses every psychological trick to break the will of an audience. He makes use of all the conditions which have made in the German people a longing for submission; their anxieties, their feelings of loneliness (9). He understands his subjects because they are so like himself (4).

Closely related to his attitude toward power, and one of the basic elements of Hitler's personality structure, is a deeply-rooted need for aggression, destruction, brutality. It was with him in phantasy, at least in childhood (9), and there is evidence of it from his days in Vienna (7). We know; too (9) that the outbreak of the first great war was a tremendously thrilling experience for him. Since the

10. It is interesting to note, that the war against Britain appears only to have broken out because Hitler was convinced that she would not and could not resist the strength of the German armed forces.

war we have seen his adoption of so-called "communist" methods of dealing with hecklers (9), the murder of his close friends, his brutality toward the Jews, his destruction of one small nation after another, and his more recent major war against the rest of the world. But this element of his personality is so patent that it hardly needs documenting.

Hitler's attitude toward the Jews and toward Race.

Anti-Semitism is not an uncommon thing and Europe has a long history of it, but, as has been pointed out, "in the case of Hitler, the Jew has been elevated, so to speak, to a degree of evilness which he had" never before obtained" (10, 8). That this hatred is of a more than usual pathological nature is suggested by the morbid connection which Hitler makes between the Jew and disease, blood diseases, syphilis (9), and filthy excrescences of all sorts. The Jew, in fact, is not even a beast, he is a creature outside of nature (16). He is at the root of all things evil, not only in Germany but elsewhere, and only through his destruction may the world be saved.

It is at this point, too, that Hitler's feelings about race find expression. For him there is an inner, emotional connection between sex, syphilis, blood impurity, Jewishness and the degeneration of pure, healthy and virile racial strains. Like the need for aggression, his fear of the tainting of blood is a major element in Hitler's personality structure.

Hitler's Attitude Toward Sex.

That Hitler's attitude toward sex is pathological is already clear from what has been said above. The best sources we have do not, however, tell us explicitly what it is that is wrong with Hitler's sex life. From the fact that his close associate, Röhm, as well as many of the early Nazis, were homosexuals, it has been a matter of gossip that Hitler, too, is affected in this way. All reliable sources, however, deny that there is any evidence whatever for such an idea (8). In fact, Hitler appears to have no close men friends, no intimates at all. Röhm was the only one whom he addressed with the intimate, "du" (5) and it is reported that no one has succeeded, since the latter's death, to such a position of intimacy.

In regard to women, the reports are conflicting. Most of the recent books by newspaper men (e.g, 5) stress Hitler's' asceticism, his disinterest in women. However, Heiden (8) documents his love affairs, and Henisch (7) Strasser (18), and Rauschning (15) have much to say about his attitude towards the opposite sex. As far as can be ascertained, it is completely lacking in respect, is contemptuous (7) and is opportunistic (18; 16), and in the actual sexual relationship there is something of a perverse nature along with a peculiar enslavement to the partner of his choice (8). It is certain that many women find Hitler fascinating (16; 7) and that he likes their company, but it is also true that he has never married, and in every love affair the break was made, not by Hitler, but by the lady concerned (8). In one case, that of his niece, Geli, there was real tragedy involved for either he murdered her in a fit of passion, according to Strasser's evidence (18), or he so abused and upset her that she committed suicide (8). Finally, one must mention again his frenzied outburst against syphilis in Mein Kampf (9), as if the whole German nation was a vast, putrefying hotbed of this loathsome disease. Heiden's statement (8) that "there is something wrong" with Hitler's sex life is surely an eloquent understatement.

Hitler's Need to Talk.

This rather obvious need is worth noting at this point, after what has just been said above. (11) Ever since Hitler's discovery of his facility as a speaker, his own people and the world have been deluged with his words. The number of speeches is large, varying in length from one and a half to two hours, though there are several of three and even four hours' duration. In private, Hitler seldom converses, for each individual whom he addresses is a new audience to be harangued. In his moments of depression he must talk to prove to himself his own strength and in moments of exaltation, to dominate others (16).

Hitler's Attitude Towards Art.

Though Hitler's father intended him to be a civil servant, he himself craved to be an artist and his failure to be recognized as such by the Vienna school was one of his most traumatic experiences (9). As Führer, his interest in .art continues and he shows distinctly favorable attitudes towards music, painting, and architecture.

11. From the analytic point of view, this may well be interpreted as a compensation for sexual difficulties.

As is well known, Wagner is Hitler's favorite - we might almost say only - composer. At twelve he was captivated by Lohengrin (9); at nineteen, in Vienna, he was championing the merit of Wagner as against Mozart (7), and as Führer he has seen Die Meistersinger over a hundred times (19). He knows all of Wagner's scores (19) and in their rendition he gets emotional release and inspiration for his actions. His savior complex; feelings about sex, race purity; his attitudes toward food and drink, all find stimulus and reinforcement in the plots, persons and themes of his favorite composer. It is interesting, for example, that Hitler has chosen Nuremberg, the town which Wagner personified in Hans Sachs, as the official site of the meeting of the annual Nazi Party Congress (19).

Wagner's Influence over Hitler extends beyond the realm of music to that of literature. Among the Führer's' favorite readings are Wagner's political writings, and, consciously or unconsciously, he has copied Wagner's turgid and bombastic manner with a resulting style which, according to Heiden, often transforms "a living sentence into a confused heap of bony, indigestible word-art." (8, 308).

In the field of painting there are two matters to consider - Hitler's own work and his attitude towards the work of others. As regards the former, we have evidence that during his Vienna days Hitler showed little ability except for copying the paintings of others (7). Some of the works that are extant, however, display some flair for organization and color, though there is nothing original. Many of his paintings show a preoccupation with architecture, old ruins and with empty, desolate places – few of them contain people. The somewhat hackneyed designs of the party badge and flag give further evidence of lack of originality. As regards the painting of others, Hitler has surrounded himself with military pictures of all sorts and with portraits of very liberal and explicit nudes (13; 18). At his command, German art has been purged of its modernism, and classic qualities are stressed instead.

It is in architecture that Hitler's artistic interest finds its greatest outlet. He spends a great deal of time over architect's designs, and all important German buildings and monuments must be approved by him. Massiveness, expansiveness, size and classic design are the qualities which Hitler stresses and approves in the buildings of the new Germany. His seventy-five foot broad motor roads, the conference grounds at Nuremberg, and his retreat at Berchtesgaden are all examples of these emphases.

Hitler's Ascetic Qualities.

Hitler's ascetic qualities are popularly known and are substantiated by many writers (5; 13). Hitler himself, according to Rauschning (16), credits his vegetarianism and his abstinence from tobacco and alcohol to Wagner's Influence. He ascribes much of the decay of civilization to abdominal poisoning through excesses. This asceticism of Hitler's is all the more striking among a people who, on the whole, are heavy eaters and fond of drinking. It is worthy of note, however, that at times Hitler is not averse to certain types of over- indulgence. He is for example, excessively fond of sweets, sweetmeats and pastry (7; 15), and will consume them in large quantities.

Hitler's Peculiar Abilities.

Hitler, the uneducated, is nevertheless a man of unusual ability, particularly in certain areas where formal education is of little value and even in areas where it is supposed to be important. More than once we find those who know him (e.g., Rauschning (16) stressing his extraordinary ability to take a complicated problem and reduce it to very simple terms. It is hardly necessary to document Hitler's ability to understand and make use of the weaknesses of his opponents; his ability to divide them and strike them one by one; his sense of timing so as to strike at the most opportune moment. It is certain, however, that these abilities of Hitler's have definite limitations. Hitler has become more and more insulated (16) from contact with what is actually occurring and thus has insufficient or incorrect data on which to base his decisions. Moreover, his own frame of reference is an unsatisfactory guide to an understanding of peoples outside the European milieu. Ha has consequently frequently misunderstood both British and American points of view with unhappy results to his own program of expansion.

Overt Evidence of Maladjustment.

Certain facts symptomatic of maladjustment have already been mentioned, such as his peculiar relationship to women. Here there have to be added others of a less specific nature. Hitler suffers from severe insomnia and when he does sleep he has violent nightmares (16). At times he suffers from hallucinations, often hearing voices on his long solitary walks (16). He has an excessive fear of poisoning and takes extreme precautions to guard against it both in his food and in his bedroom (16). Here the bed must be made only in one specific way (16). He cannot work steadily, but with explosive outbursts of activity, or not at all (16; 8). Even the smallest decision demands great effort and he has to work himself up to it. When thwarted, he will break out into an hysterical tantrum, scolding in high-pitched tones, foaming at the mouth, and stamping with uncontrolled fury (16). On several occasions, when an important speech was due, he has stood silent before his audience and then walked out on them (16). In the case of at least one international broadcast he was suddenly and inexplicably cut off the air. Finally, there is Hitler's threat to commit suicide if the Nazi party is destroyed or the plans of the German Reich fail. (6)

THE SOURCES OF HITLER'S MALADJUSTMENTS

The Sources of Hitler's Aggressive and Submissive Traits.

The schizoid temperament, one such as Hitler's, which combines both a sensitive, shy, and indrawn nature with inhibitions of feeling toward others, and at the same time, in way of compensation; violent aggressiveness, callousness and brutality, from one point of view of constitutional psychology is usually associated with a particular type of physique. It is difficult from the sort of photograph available to classify Hitler's physique accurately. He probably falls in Kretschmer's athletic group, though verging on the pyknic (11). This would place him in the schizophrenic group of temperaments. In terms of Sheldon's system, he is probably classifiable as a 443 with a considerable degree of gynandromorphy, that is, an essentially masculine body but one showing feminine characteristics also (17). Probably more important, however, is the social milieu and the family situation in which Hitler grew up. In a strongly patriarchal society, his father was particularly aggressive and probably brutal toward his son, Adolph. This would produce an individual both very submissive to authority and at the same time, boiling over with rebelliousness to it. Further, we know of the extreme attachment which Hitler had for his mother. If, as seems most likely, he has never outgrown this (12), there might be a protest in his nature against this enslavement, which in turn might give rise to a deep unconscious hatred – a possible source of frightful, unconscious rage. (13) Finally, the consistent failure to achieve his artistic ambitions, his loneliness and poverty in Vienna, his failure to arrive at any higher status than that of corporal in his beloved army (8), all must have stimulated in highest degree whatever original tendency there wad toward brutality and destructiveness.

12. Note Hitler's frequent and unusual use of the word Motherland for Germany. (9).

13. Hitler's hatred of meat and love of sweets is said to be often found in cases harboring an unconscious hate of the mother (15).

The Sources of Hitler's Anti-Semitism.

Anti- Semitism was part of the social milieu in which Hitler grew up. He admits himself (9) that he avoided the only Jewish boy at school and it is known that anti-Semitism and asceticism were strong in Catholic, rural communities in Europe. In Vienna, of course, Hitler came in contact with violent, anti-Semitic literature and it is at this period that he claims his deep-rooted hatred for the Jews was born (9).

The pathological strength of this hatred suggests that there were certain psychological as well as cultural reasons for it. What they were we can only surmise, but we can list certain possibilities. We know that the name Hitler is a common Jewish one (8); that Adolf was teased about his Jewish appearance in Vienna. **(14)** There is, too, the

14. It is interesting that Hitler's description of the first Jew to arouse his hatred is almost word for word the same as Hanisch's description of Hitler in Vienna (7).

mystery of Alois Hitler's true parentage, which his son may have known. We also know that many of the people who helped him, gave him food and bought his paintings were Jews. **(15)** To have to accept kindnesses from people he disliked would not add to his love of them. But there must be more to it than this, for Hitler's anti-Semitism la bound up with his morbid concern with syphilis and phobia over contamination of the blood of the German race. This, therefore, leads to a discussion of Hitler's theories.

Sources of Hitler's Theories of Race and Blood.

The concept of the superiority of the Aryan race is, of course, not new with Hitler. Its great exponent was Houston Stewart Chamberlain. In the writings of Wagner also the same conception is exalted. But the constant repetition of the idea of blood – pure blood and untainted blood - which occurs in Mein Kampf calls for a more than purely cultural explanation.

This is suggested all the more forcefully because of the association which Hitler makes between impurities of blood which are due to disease (syphilis), and impurities in the blood of a superior race due to mixture with a racially inferior stock;

15. His rejection of the Jew may also stem from the rejection within himself of the passive, gentle elements which are prominent in Hebrew-Christian thought.

further to the fact that he points to the Jews as the source of both.

Now it is known that syphilo-phobia often has its roots in the childhood discovery of the nature of sexual congress between the parents. With a father who was an illegitimate - and possibly of Jewish origin (16) - and a strong mother fixation, such a discovery by the child Adolph may well have laid the basis of a syphilo-phobia, which some adventure with a Jewish prostitute in Vienna fanned to a full flame. (17) Terrified by the fear of his own infection, all the hatred in his being is then directed toward the Jews.

ONE POSSIBLE PSYCHOLOGICAL INTERPRETATION

Hitler's personality structure, though falling within the normal range, may now be described as of the paranoid type, with delusions of persecution and of grandeur. This stems from a sado-masochistic split in his personality (4). Integral with these alternating and opposed elements in his personality are his fear of infection, the identification of the Jews as the source of that infection, and some derangement of the sexual function which makes his relations to the opposite sex abnormal in nature.

16. The name Hitler is Jewish, as was pointed out.

17. This is mere conjecture and must be treated as such. But it is the sort of explanation which fits known psychological facts.

The drama and tragedy of Hitler's life are the projection onto the world of his own inner conflicts and his attempts to solve them. The split in Hitler's personality seems clearly to-be due to his identification both with his mother, whom he passionately loved, and with his father, whom he hated and feared. This dual and contradictory identification (the one is gentle, passive, feminine; the other brutal, aggressive, masculine) results, whenever Hitler is playing the aggressive role, also in a deep hatred and contempt for his mother and love and admiration for his father. This inner conflict is projected into the world where Germany comes to represent the mother, and the Jew and - for a time - the Austrian state, the father. Just as the father is the cause of his mixed blood, the source of his domination and punishment, and of the restrictions of his own artistic development; just as in the childish interpretation of sexual congress the father attacks, strangles and infects the mother, so the Jew - international Jewish capital, etc., - encircles and restricts Germany; threatens and attacks her and infects her with impurities of blood. Out of the hatred of the father and love of the mother came the desire to save her. So Hitler becomes the savior of Germany, who cleanses her of infection, destroys her enemies, breaks their encirclement, removes every restriction upon her so that she may expand into new living space, un-cramped and un-throttled. At the same time, Hitler is cleansing himself, defending himself; casting off paternal domination and restriction.

Not only is the Father feared but he is a source of jealousy for he possesses, at least in part, the beloved mother. So he must be destroyed to permit complete possession. The destruction of the father is achieved symbolically by the destruction of the Austrian state and complete domination and possession of the mother, through gathering all Germans in a common Reich.

But the mother is not only loved but also hated. For she is weak; besides he is enslaved to her affections and she reminds him all too much, in his role as dominant father, of his own gentle, sensitive nature. So, though he depends on the German people for his position of dominance, he despises and hates them, he dominates them, and, because he fears his very love of them, he leads them into the destructiveness of war where multitudes of them are destroyed. Besides, the Jewish element in his father identification permits him to use all the so-called "Jewish" tricks of deceit, lying, violence and sudden attack to subject the German people as well as their foes.

To be dominant, aggressive, brutal is to arouse the violent protest of the other side of his nature. Only severe anxiety can come from this; nightmares and sleepless nights result. But fear is assuaged by the fiction of the demands of Fate, of Destiny, of the Folk-Soul of the German people.

The denouement of the drama approaches at every aggressive step. The fiction of the command of Fate only holds as long as there is success - greater and greater success to assuage the mounting feelings of anxiety and guilt. Aggression, therefore, has a limit; it cannot go beyond the highest point of success.

When that is reached, the personality may collapse under the flood of its own guilt feelings. **(18)** It is, therefore, quite possible that Hilter will do away with himself at whatever moment German defeat becomes sufficient enough to destroy the fiction of Fate which has shielded him from the violence of his own guilt. He may then turn upon himself the destructiveness which so long has been channeled toward his people and their neighbors.

18. That Hitler is partly conscious of this we know from his own threats of suicide and references to dying for the German people. (9).

BIBLIOGRAPHY

1. Bloch, E. **MY PATIENT HITLER**.
Collier's, March 15, 1941.

2. Dodd, M. **THROUGH EMBESSY EYES**.
New York Harcourt, Brace, 1939.

3. Farago, L. **GERMAN PSYCHOLOGICAL WARFARE** New York: Committee on National Morale, 1941.

4. Frome, E. **ESCAPE FROM FREEDOM.**
New York: Farrar & Rinehart, 1941.

5. Gunther, J. **INSIDE EUROPE.**
New York and London: Hamper, 1935.

6. Haffner, S. **GERMANY: JEKYLL AND HYDE.** London: Secker & Warburn, 1940.

7. Hanisch, R. **I WAS HITLER'S BUDDY.** New Republic, April 5, 1959.

8. Heiden, K. **HITLER, A BIOGRAPHY**. London: Constable, 1955.

9. Hitler, A. **MEIN KAMPF.** New York: Reynal & Hitchcock, 1939.

10. Hitler, A. **MY NEW ORDER.** New York: Reynal & Hitchcock, 1941.

11. Kretschmer, E. **PHYSIQUE AND CHARACTER.** New York: Harcourt, Brace, 1925.

12. Krueger, K. **INSIDE HITLER** New York: Avalon Press,1941.

13. Lewis, W. **HITLER-CULT** London: Dent, 1939.

14. Life, June 23, 1941.

15. Medicus. **A PSYCHIATRIST LOOKS AT HITLER.** New Republic, April 26, 1939.

16. Rauschning,,H . **HITLER'SPEAKS.** London: Butterworth, 1939.

17. Sheldon,,W,H. **THE VARIETIES OF HUMAN PHYSIQUE.**
New York: Harper, 1940.

18. Strasser, O. **HITLER AND I.**
Boston: Houghton Mifflin 1940.

19. Viereck, P. **METAPOLITICS.**
New York: Knopf, 1941.

SECTION III

Detailed Analysis of Hitler's Personality.

(Written especially for psychologists and
psychiatrists)

FOREWORD TO THE DETAILED ANALYSIS

In writing this analysis of Hitler's personality, the
use of certain technical words was unavoidable.
Although I have attempted to follow as simple and
intelligible a form as possible, I could not, without
much circumlocution and vagueness, get along
without three terms:

Need (roughly synonymous with Drive, impulse,
tendency, purpose, instinct), This is a force within
the subject (i.e., the individual whose behavior is
being studied) which inclines him to strive toward a
certain goal, the attainment of which reduces
momentarily the tension of the need. Needs vary in
kind and in strength,

Press (plural: press). This is a force emanating
from an object (usually a person) in the environ-
ment, which is directed toward the subject. A press
(for the subject) is the need or drive in the object,
which, if successful, would harm or benefit him.
Press vary in kind and in strength.

Cathexis. This is the power of an object to arouse
feelings of liking (positive cathexis) or of disliking
(negative cathexis) in the subject. It is also

permissible to say that the subject "positively cathects" or simply "cathects" (values, admires, loves) one object; or that he "negatively cathects (depredates, scorns, fears, hates) another. The cathexis (potency) of objects - their ability to evoke behavior in the subject - can vary in kind (positive or negative) or in strength.

1. STATEMENT OF THE PROBLEM

Thirty years ago Hitler was a common bum, an unemployed non-entity; a derelict of the polyglot society that was Vienna.. "It was a miserable life," his pal, Hanisch, has written, "and I once asked him what he was really waiting for. He answered: 'I don't know myself.' I have never seen such helpless letting-down in distress."

Twenty years later Hitler was dictator of all Germany. He was not waiting for anything, but demanding and getting all that a boundlessly ambitious man could want. Many people thought that they had never seen such resolute confidence in victory.

Three years ago, at the age of fifty-one, Hitler was the most powerful and successful individual on earth; on the one hand, the most worshipped; on the other, the most despised. In Germany he was virtually a demigod; he had unlimited power; he was always right; he could do no wrong; he was the savior of the Vaterland, the conqueror of Europe; the divinely appointed prophet of a new era. There was a Hitler Strasse or a Hitler Platz in every town.

"Heil Hitler" was the conventional greeting for acquaintances. The man's picture was prominently displayed in every public building; in every railroad station; in millions of homes. His autobiography was accepted as the Bible of a revolutionary folk religion. Hitler was compared to Christ.

The man is chiefly interesting as a force that has affected the lives of more people on this globe than any man in history, aided, to be sure, by new and miraculous instruments of communication. How was it possible for a man so insignificant in stature and appearance, so deficient in bodily strength and emotional control, so lacking in intellectual attainments - how was it possible for such a man to succeed where the mightiest Germans of the past had failed? What kind of a man is this Hitler? What are his chief abilities and disabilities? What conditions in Germany were conducive to his meteoric rise to power? What is he likely to do next? And, if the Allies get their hands on him, how can he be treated so that he will never rise again as a legendary figure to instigate another Satanic revolution against culture? These are among the questions that have been faced in this paper.

The aspects of Hitler's personality that especially require explanation are these: the intensity of the man's dedication to the creation of an ideal; the nature of his life-drama, or Mission, as he conceives it; the fanaticism of his sentiments, *pro* - Power, Glory, Dictatorship, Militarism, Brutality, the Aggressive Instinct, Nationalism, Purity of Blood; and the fanaticism of his sentiments, *con* –

Weakness, Indecision, Tolerance, Compassion, Peace, National Debate, Democracy, Bolshevism, the Acquisitive Instinct, Materialism, Capitalism, the Jewish Race, Christianity. Also of interest are: the nature of his oratorical power over the emotions of the masses; his painting and architectural interests; the vagaries of his sex instinct and the significance of his neurotic and psychotic symptoms,

II. PHYSICAL CONSTITUTION

1. Physique

A point of fundamental importance is the large gynic (feminine) component in Hitler's constitution.

His hips are wide and his shoulders relatively narrow. His muscles are flabby, his legs thin and spindly, the latter being hidden in the past by heavy boots and more recently by long trousers. He is hollow chested, and in the throes of passionate speech his voice sometimes breaks into shrill falsetto.

In contrast to his masculine ideal for German youth, Hitler's physical strength and agility are definitely below the average. He was frail as a child, never labored in the fields; never played rough games. He has long, tapering, sensitive fingers. In Vienna, he was too weak to be employed on construction jobs and before the outbreak of world War I, was rejected by the Austrian Army as permanently disqualified for service. He was discouraged, after one attempt, to ride a horse, and in the lest twenty years his exercise has been limited to short walks. Some informants say that he is physically incapable of normal sexual relations. His movements have been described as womanish – a dainty, lady-like way of walking (when not assuming a military carriage in public); effeminate gestures of his arms; a peculiar, graceless ineptitude reminiscent of a girl throwing a baseball.

2. Medical and Psychiatric History

Hitler has suffered from nervous gastritis, or indigestion, for many years. This is probably a psychosomatic syndrome; part and parcel of his general neuroticism.

A German psychiatrist who examined Hitler's medical record in World War I has reported that the diagnosis of his condition was hysterical blindness. In other words, he did not suffer from mustard gas poisoning, as publicly stated, but from a war neurosis. It has also been said that he was not only blind but dumb, and (according to one informant), deaf.

Some years ago a benign polyp was removed from a vocal chord.

Hitler is a victim of temper tantrums which have increased in intensity and frequency during the last ten years. A typical seizure consists of:

1. Pacing, shouting, cursing, blaming, accusations

of treachery and betrayal.

2. Weeping and exhibitions of self-pity, and;

3. Falling on the floor, foaming at the mouth, biting the carpet.

The man has some control over these epileptiform attacks, using them to get his own way with his close associates.

Hitler also suffers from agitated depressions, affrighting nightmares, hypochondriacal states in which he fears that he will be poisoned or die from cancer of the stomach.

III. APPEARANCE AND EXPRESSIVE ATTITUDES

The most significant fact about Hitler's appearance is its utter insignificance. He is the prototype of the little man; an unnecessary duplicate, apparently, that one would never turn to look at twice. For ten years, notwithstanding, Germans have been gazing at him and, spellbound, seen the magnetic figure of one who could have said and done what Hitler has said and done.

Comments have chiefly centered on Hitler's eyes and his hands. Although his greyish-blue eyes are usually staring and dead - impersonal and unseeing - at times he looks a man or a woman straight in the face with a fixed, unwavering gaze that has been described as positively hypnotic. Behind the habitual vacancy of expression some discern an intense flame of passionate dedication. His hands are strikingly well-shaped and expressive, and in haranguing an audience they are used to good effect.

In all other respects, Hitler's appearance is totally lacking in distinction. His features are soft, his cheeks callow and puffy; his handshake is loose, his palms moist and clammy. Such features can hardly he appreciated by the average visitor as evidences of an Iron Man.

In his reactions to the world, Hitler plays many parts. There is the **Expressionless Hitler,** like a dummy standing with upraised hand in the front of a six-wheeled motorcar that moves at a slow pace down the great avenue between serried ranks of shouting, worshipful adherents. There is the **Embarrassed Hitler,** ill at ease, even subservient, in the presence of a stranger, an aristocrat, a great general or a king (as on his visit to Italy). There is the **Gracious Hitler,** the soft, good-natured Austrian; gentle, informal and even modest, welcoming friendly admirers at his villa; as well as the **Sentimental Hitler,** weeping over a dead canary. Then there is the **Tactical Hitler,** who comes in at the critical moment with the daringly right decision; and the **Mystical Hitler,** hinting of a thousand years of superiority for the German folk; the **Possessed Hitler,** shrieking with fanatical fury as he exhorts the masses; the **Hysterical Hitler,** rolling on the carpet or shaking with terror as he wakes from a nightmare; the **Apathetic Hitler,** limp, indolent and indecisive; and at all times, the **Soapbox Hitler,** ready to go off half-cocked on a long tirade even though he is addressing a single individual. Of all these, it is the Tactical Hitler, the Mystical Hitler and the Possessed Hitler which have been chiefly instrumental in winning the position he now holds. It is because of these powerful inhabitants of his being that people have accepted and tolerated the less appealing or less bearable inhabitants.

IV: Past History

Chronology*

1837: Marie Anna Schicklgruber has an illegitimate son, Alois,- born in Strones, near Spital.
Johann Georg Hiedler (Hitler) m. Marie Anna Schicklgruber

1850: Birth of Klara Poelzl in Spital.

1877 :Jan.6; Alois Schicklgruber legitimized as Alois Hitler. Alois Hitler m. Anna Glasl-Horer (14 years older).

1883: Death of Anna Glasl-Horer. in Braunau

1883: Alois Hitler m. Franziska Matzelberger.

ca. 1885: Birth of Alois Hitler Jr., 2 months after marriage.

1884: Birth of Angela Hitler.

1884: Death of Franziska Matzelberger.

1865; Jan. 7: Alois Hitler (47 years.) m. Klara Poelzl.
Birth of two children who die in. infancy.

1889; Apr 20: Birth of Adolf Hitler in Braunau.
Family move to Passau (Bavaria) on Austrian border.

ca. 1893: Alois Hitler retires on a pension.
Family moves to Lambach (24 miles from Linz);
Catholic Convent.

ca. 1896 Birth of Paula Hitler.

ca. 1900 Family move to Leonding (suburb of linz);
Technical School

1903: Jan. 3; Death of Alois Hitler
Family move o Linz.

1904-5: Adolf Hitler attends school in Steyr.

1907: Oct; Hitler fails to pass examination of
Academy of Arts, Vienna.

1907: Dec. 21; Klara Hitler dies. (A. H. Is 18 years
old).

1908: Jan; A.H. moves to Vienna.

1908: Oct:. A. H. fails a second time to pass
examination of Academy of Arts.

1913: A. H. moves to Munich.

* **Not all these dates are reliable.** Most of the
early ones are from Gunther's INSIDE EUROPE.

A. Childhood and Adolescence: 1889-1907

I. Family Relations

1. <u>Father</u>

Some of the confusion that has arisen in regard to Hitler's forebears disappears as soon as we realize the name Hitler has been variously spelled; Hidler, Hiedler, Buettler - by different members of the same illiterate peasant family. Adolf Hitler's grandparents were both descended from one Hitler (father's grandfather and mother's great-grandfather), an inhabitant of the culturally backward Waldviertel district, upper Austria.

Marshal Hindenburg

Alois Hitler
(Hitler's Father)
Note
resemblance
to Hindenburg

Family History and Personality of Father

The chief facts about Alois Hitler which have bearing on our analysis are these:

(a) According to an inquiry ordered by the Austrian Chancellor, Dollfuss, Maria Anna Schicklegruber became pregnant during her employment as a servant in a Jewish Viennese family. For this reason she was sent back to her home in the country.

If this is true, Alois Hitler may have been half Jewish, The fact that he selected a Jew, Herr Prinz of Vienna, to be the godfather of his son Adolf, is in line with this hypothesis.

(b) In any event, Alois Hitler was illegitimate and as such was no doubt made to suffer the contempt of the little community, Spital, in which he was reared. Perhaps it was for this reason that he left his home at an early age to seek his fortune in Vienna.

(c) Alois Hitler started life as a simple cobbler but finally improved his status by becoming a customs official. For a time he patrolled the German-Austrian border, was known as a "man-hunter". He was very proud of this position, believing that it entitled him to lord it over those of the class that had once scorned him.

(d) In appearance, Alois Hitler resembled Marshal Hindenburg. He had a walrus moustache, under which protruded a sullen and arrogant lower lip. He wore a uniform, his badge of status; and as a border patrolman carried a revolver on his person. He smoked and ran after women. It is said that he frequented the village pub and enjoyed nothing so much as recounting his accomplishments to a receptive auditory. He was a coarse man, with boasts and curses forever on his tongue. He died of apoplexy.

(e) He was twenty-three years older than his wife, a peasant girl who had once served as a maid in the house of his first wife. Thus, the father's greater age, his higher social status, the traditional prerogatives of the husband in the German family, the man's over-weening pride — all supported him in maintaining a master-servant relationship with his wife. Frau Hitler was nervous, mild, devoted and submissive. In his own home, Alois Hitler was a tyrant.

(f) In his treatment of his son, Adolf, it is said that the father was stern and harsh. Physical punishments were frequent. He seems to have looked on his son as a weakling; a good-for-nothing, moonstruck dreamer. At times, perhaps, his vanity imagined a successful career for the boy, which would still further lift the family status, and so when young Adolf announced his intention to be an artist the father, perceiving the frustration of his dream, put his foot down — *"An artist, no, never as long as I live."* (K.K. 14).

(g) There is some doubt about the complexion of Alois Hitler's political sentiments. Hanisch reports that "Hitler heard from his father only praise of Germany and all the faults of Austria," but, according to Holden, more reliable informants claim that the father, though full of complaints and criticisms of the government he served, was by no means a German nationalist. They say he favored Austria against Germany.

(h) It is not unlikely that Hitler, in writing his sketch of the typical lower class home, drew upon his personal experiences, and if this is true, the following passages give us an interesting side-light on the character of the father:

(i) But things end badly, indeed, when the man from the very start goes his own way (Alois Hitler 'ran after other women') and the wife, for the sake of her children, stands up against him. Quarreling and nagging set in, and in the same measure in which the husband becomes estranged from his wife, he becomes familiar with alcohol…"When he finally comes home on Sunday or Monday night, drunk and brutal, but always without a last cent and penny, then God have mercy on the scenes which follow. I witnessed all of this personally in hundreds of scenes and at the beginning with both disgust and indignation." (M.K: 38-38).

The other things the little fellow hears at home do not tend to further his respect for his surroundings. Not a single shred is left for humanity, not a single institution is left un-attacked, starting with the teacher up to the head of the State, be it religion, or morality as such, be it the State or Society - no matter which - everything is abused, everything is pulled down in the nastiest manner into the filth of a depraved mentality. (M..K. 43).

(i) <u>Relations to Father</u>

There are reasons to believe that the boy Adolf was very much afraid of his father in his early years, that he was timid and submissive in his presence; but when he was out of reach of his father's immense authority (when his father was out of the house or when the boy was at school under less severe disciplinarians) he was often unruly and defiant. He had no respect for a lenient system of government.

Not until he was eleven did Adolf dare to oppose his father. Here the issue was the selection of his vocation. Herr Hitler wanted his son to follow in his footsteps and become a State official, but the boy decided he wanted to be an artist. Of this conflict between father and son, Hitler writes:

(i) His domineering: nature, the result of a life-long struggle for existence, would have thought it unbearable to leave the ultimate decision to a boy who, in his opinion, was inexperienced and irresponsible. (M.K* 11).

(ii) No matter how firm and determined my father might be in carrying out his plans and intentions, once made, his son was just as stubborn and obstinate. (M.K. 12).

(iii) …he opposed me with the resoluteness of his entire nature...the old man became embittered, and, much as I loved him, the same was true of myself…and now the old man relentlessly began to enforce his authority. (M.K. 13-14).

It is obvious from these and other passages, as well as from local hearsay, that the relations of Adolf and his parent from 1900-1903 (when the father died) were exceedingly stormy. It was a classical father-son conflict.

(J) Note: Hitler's attitude to old men. In many places, in MEIN KAMPF and in some of his recorded conversations, Hitler speaks of old men in a derogatory and contemptuous manner. It is often very suggestive of what might have been his sentiments towards his sixty-year-old father (twenty-three years older than his mother). The following quotations might be cited in illustration:

(i) Rauschning: Everywhere, Hitler complained there were nothing but sterile old men in their second childhood, who bragged of their technical knowledge and had lost their sound common sense.

(ii) Hitler quoted by Heiden: My great adversary, Reichspraisident von Hindenburg, is today eighty-five years of age. I am forty-three and, I feel, in perfect health. And nothing will happen to me, for I am clearly conscious of the great task which Providence has assigned to me.

2. <u>Mother</u>

(a) <u>Personality of Mother</u>

The pertinent facts are these; Klara Poelzl was an exemplary housekeeper. Her home was always spotlessly clean, everything had its place, not a speck of dust on the furniture. She had a gentle nature. Her relatively young age, her docile character, her years of domestic service — all inclined her to compliance and Christian resignation. The trials and tribulations of life with an irascible husband resulted in a permanent attitude of abnegation. Toward her son, Adolf, she was ever devoted, catering to his whims to the point of spoiling him. She it was who encouraged his artistic ambitions.

The mother was operated on for cancer of the breast in the summer of 1907 and died within six months. It is very likely that the disease was marked by ulcerations of the chest wall and metastasis in the lungs.

Hitler's Mother

(b) <u>Relations to Mother</u>

Hitler has written very little and said nothing publicly about his mother, but the few scraps obtained suggest many youthful years of loving dependence upon her. Hitler speaks of:

(i) …the mother devoting herself to the cares of the household looking after her children with eternally the same loving kindness. (M.K. 6).

(ii) For three or four of the five years between his father's and his mother's deaths, Adolf Hitler idled away a good deal of his time as the apple of his mother's eye. She allowed him to drop his studies at the Realschule; she encouraged him in his ambitions to be a painter; she yielded to his every wish. During these years, it is reported, the relationship between mother and son was marked by reciprocal adoration. Hitler's amazing self-assurance, (at most times) can be attributed in part to the impression of these years when at the age of thirteen his father died and he succeeded to the power and became the little dictator of the family. His older brother, Alois, had left by this time, and he was the only male in a household of four. "These were my happiest days; they seemed like a dream to me, and they were." (M.K. 25).

(iii) Hitler writes; "My mother's death...was a terrible shock to me...I loved my mother."

(iv) Dr. Bloch reports that Adolf cried when he heard of his mother's sufferings at operation and later, at her death, exhibited great grief. The Doctor has never seen anyone so prostrate with sorrow. After her burial in the Catholic cemetery, Adolf stayed by her grave long after the others had departed.

(v) Hitler wore the picture of his mother over his breast in the field during World War One.

(vi) That the mother-child relationship was a compelling, though rejected, pattern for Hitler may be surmised from (1) his attachment to "substitute mothers" during his post-war years (2) his frequent use of mother imagery in speaking and writing and (3) his selection of pictures of Madonna and child to decorate his rooms.

Corner of big room at Berchtesgaden. Painting of Madonna and Child over mantel.

From these and other bits of evidence we can conclude that Hitler loved his mother and hated his father; that he had an Oedipus Complex, in other words. But, as we shall soon see, this can explain only one phase of his relationship to his parents.

(c) <u>Siblings</u>

It is certain that there were two older children in the

household during Adolf's early years. The father had been married twice before; there was a half-brother, Alois Hitler, Jr., and a half-sister, Angela Hitler. We know nothing of Hitler's relationship to the former (who much later turned up in Berlin as proprietor of a restaurant). The half-sister, Angela, married Herr Raubal, an official in the tax bureau at Linz. Later she managed a restaurant for Jewish students at the University of Vienna. For some years she was Hitler's house-keeper at Berchtesgaden, until she married Professor Martin Hamnizsch of Dresden, where she now lives.

(i) Several informants have stated that there is a younger sister, Paula, born when Adolf was about seven years old. Consequently, he must have experienced the press Birth of Sibling during his childhood. This younger sister, it seems, is a very peculiar, reclusive person who now lives in Vienna. It has been said that she had affairs with several men in turn, one of whom was a Jew. It is believed that she is mentally retarded.

(ii) There are reports of two children who died in infancy before Adolf was born. One of these may have been Edmund, or Gustaf, mentioned by some informants.

3. <u>Boyhood Reactions, Activities and Interests</u>

Very little reliable information exists as to Hitler's childhood. Most informants, however, agree on the following points:

(a) Physical Weakness: Adolf was a frail lad - thin and pale. He did not participate in any athletics or enjoy hard physical exercise. He was sensitive and liked to be with his mother, look at books, sketch landscapes or take walks by himself. He liked to daydream about Germany's wars, but he did nothing to fit himself to be a soldier. When he tired of school (ashamed of his inferiority in scholarship), he became nervously sick (feigned lung trouble), and his mother permitted him to drop out and stay at home.

(b) Low Tolerance of Frustration: One can be certain that, as a child. Adolf reacted violently to frustration. He undoubtedly had temper tantrums which were rewarded by his mother's ready compliance to his wishes. (This was his way of "courting the soul of the common people".) He was also finicky about food, we can be sure.

(c) <u>Rebelliousness and Repeated Aggression.</u>

At home, discipline was capricious. His father was

often unusually severe, his mother inordinately lenient. As a result, he developed no steady and consistent character. He alternated between subservience (to placate his father) and unruliness.

(i) Lansing: His first teacher recalled…that he was a quarrelsome, stubborn lad who smoked cigarettes and cigar stubs collected from the gutter or begged from roisterers in the public houses.

(ii) Hanish reports that Hitler told him that the people of the Innviertel were great brawlers and that, as a boy, he used to love to watch their fights. Also, that he used to enjoy visiting a fine exhibition in Linz of deadly weapons. What others abhorred appealed to him. (N.B., Here is fair evidence of repressed aggression (sadism) during boyhood.)

(iii) Hitler, as a mere boy of ten, became passionately interested in reading about the "amazingly victorious campaigns of the heroic German armies during the Franco-Prussian War." Soon this had become "my greatest spiritual experience." (M.K. 8).

(iv) I raved more and more about everything connected with war or militarism. (M.K. 8).

(v) A careful examination of the first chapter of

MEIN KAMPF will convince any psychologically trained reader that Adolf's vigorous advocacy of the cause of Germany as opposed to that of Austria from the age of eleven onward represented a legitimate substitute for his repressed rebellion against his father. Inspired by his history teacher, Professor Poetsch (father-surrogate), and a long line of German military heroes, the boy could give vent to his pent-up resentment by publicly proclaiming his devotion to the German Reich of Bismark and vehemently denouncing the authority of Austria (symbol of his father). In MEIN KAMPF Hitler writes at length of his possession of:

(vi) …an intense love for my native German-Austrian country and a bitter hatred against the 'Austrian' State. (M.K. 22-23).

Speaking of the youthful Nationalist movement that he joined, he writes:

(vii) ...it is rebellious; it wears the forbidden emblem of its own nationality and rejoices in being punished or even in being beaten for wearing that emblem...the greeting was 'Heil' and 'Deutschland uber alles' was preferred to the imperial anthem, despite warnings and punishments. (M.K. 16).

It was during these days that he first began to play

the role of a young agitator.

(viii) I believe that, even then, my ability for making speeches was trained by the more or less stirring discussions with my comrades…For obvious reasons my father could not appreciate the talent for oratory of his quarrelsome son. (M.K. 7).

The boy's ideas of greatest glory revolved round the victories of the Franco-Prussian War.

(ix) Why was it that Austria had not taken part in this war…*why not my father*? (M.K. 9). I had decidedly no sympathy for the course my father's life had taken. (M.K. 7). During the years of my unruly youth nothing had grieved me more than having been born at a time when temples of glory were only erected to merchants or State officials, (his father's profession). (M.K. 204). I, too, wanted to become 'something,' but in no event an official. (M.K. 25).

These quotations supply further evidence of Adolf's repressed hatred of his father and of the fact that negativism and willfulness had become established patterns before puberty.

(d) <u>Passivity or Illness as Means of Resistance.</u>

Hitler manifested a significant aspect of his nature when he determined to frustrate his father's intention to make a civil servant out of him. The policy he adopted was that of resistance through indolence and passivity.

(i) I was certain that as soon as my father saw my lack of progress in school ...he would let me seek the happiness of which I was dreaming. (M.K. 14).

Later, after his father's death, when he wanted to leave school, he won his mother's consent by making himself sick.

(i) Impressed by my illness my mother agreed at long last to take me out of school…(M.K. 24).

After this he spent two years of shiftless activity around the house, which set the pattern for his passive drifting and dreaming days in Vienna.

(e) Lack of Friends.

No friendships dating from boyhood have ever been mentioned and it is not likely that the boy was at all popular with his classmates. During adolescence he was said to be quiet, serious, dreamy and taciturn.

(f) Sexual Misbehavior.

A Nazi who visited Leonding much later and looked up the school records there found evidence that, at the age of eleven or twelve, Adolf had committed a serious sexual indiscretion with a little girl. For this he was punished but not expelled from school.

4. <u>Conclusions</u>

(a) <u>Hate for Father, Love for Mother, (Oedipus Complex).</u>

This has been noted and stressed by numerous psychologists and some evidence for it has been listed here. Rarely mentioned but equally important is:

(b) <u>Respect for Power of Father, Contempt for Weakness of Mother.</u>

Hitler is certainly not a typical product of the Oedipus Complex, and more can be learned about the underlying forces of his character by observing which parent he has emulated, rather than which parent he has loved. In MEIN KAMPF, he writes, "I had respected my father, but I loved my mother."

He might better have said, "I loved my mother, but I respected my father," because respect has always meant more to him than love.

(c) <u>Identification with Father.</u>

Although Hitler has not the physique or temperament of his old man, being constitutionally of another type, it is evident that he has imitated, consciously or unconsciously, many of his father's traits and none of his mother's.

(d) Adolf Hitler's will to power; his pride, aggressiveness and cult of brutality are all in keeping with what we know of the personality and conduct of Alois Hitler. The son's declaration that he has demanded nothing hut sacrifices from his adherents is certainly reminiscent of the father's attitude toward wife and children.

(i)...his son has undoubtedly inherited, among other qualities, a stubbornness similar to his own... (M.K. 14).

(e) The father's loud, boastful and perhaps drunken talk at home and at the pub (described by some informants), may well have provided his young son with an impressive model for emulation. The notion of being a village pastor had appealed to Alois Hitler and that of being an abbot appealed to his boy, no doubt for the same reason - the opportunity it afforded for oratory.

(f) Father and son each left hone to seek his fortune in Vienna. In MEIN KAMPF, there are several Indications that the image of his father's success in Vienna acted as a spur.

(i) I, too, hoped to wrest from Fate the success my father had met fifty years earlier…(M..K. 25).

(ii) And I would overcome these obstacles, always bearing in mind my father's example, who, from being a poor village boy and a cobbler's apprentice, had made his way up to the position of civil servant. (M.K. 28).

(g) Adolf Hitler sported a walrus moustache like his father's for a number of years. He finally trimmed it in imitation of a new exemplar, Feder.

(h) Adolf Hitler's invariable uniform and pistol may well have been suggested by Alois Hitler's uniform and pistol (1 (d)).

(i) It is said that Alois Hitler had a great respect for the class system; was proud of his rise in status; envied those above him and looked down upon those below him. If this is true, the father was instrumental in establishing a pattern of sentiments which was of determining importance in his son's career. Adolf Hitler has always been envious of his superiors and deferential. He has never showed any affinity for the proletariat.

(j) Adolf Hitler has hung a portrait of his father over the desk in his study.at Berchtesgaden This is a signal honor since the likeness of only three other men, Frederick the Great, Karl von Moltke and Mussolini, have been selected for inclusion in any of Hitler's rooms. There is nowhere any picture of his mother.

Hitler's Study at Berghof. Desk faces portrait of Alois Hitler.

Alois, it is said, was a smoker, a drinker and a lecher; and today his son is remarkable for his abstemiousness. Thus, in these respects the two are different. But we should not forget that Adolf used to pick up cigar butts and smoke them as a boy; he drank beer and wine. In his early Munich days, and in the last fifteen years, he has shown a good deal of interest in women.

There can be no doubt then that Hitler greatly envied and admired the power and authority of his father, and although he hated him as the tyrant who opposed and frustrated him personally, he looked on him with awe and admiration, desiring to be as he was. Speaking of his old man, the son confessed in his autobiography that "unconsciously he had sown the seeds for a future which neither he nor I would have grasped at that time." (M.K. 34). Henceforth Adolf Hitler's attention and emulation was only to be evoked by a dominating, ruthless man, and if this man1 happened to be in opposition to him, then he would hate and respect him simultaneously. Hitler's admiration for strongly enduring institutions was very similar, it seems, to his admiration for his sixty-year-old parent. He writes:

(i) …incredibly vigorous power that inhabits this age old institution (the Catholic Church).

(ii) ...he (Lueger) was disposed...to secure the favor of any existing powerful institutions, in order that he might derive from these old sources of strength the greatest possible advantage.

(k) Identification with Mother

In Hitler's constitution there is a large gynic (feminine) component and he has many feminine traits, some hidden. Consequently, in view of his avowed love for his mother, we must suppose that there was a dispositional kinship, or biological identification, between the two during the boy's earliest years. Adolf naturally and spontaneously felt the way his mother felt. This, however, was not of his own making. There is some evidence that in Hitler's mind "Germany" is a mystical conception which stands for the ideal mother--a substitute for his own imperfect mother. But there are no indications, in any event, that Hitler admired his mother or any woman who resembled her, or that he adopted any of her sentiments, or that he was even influenced by her in any important way. Hence, the conclusion is that Hitler had many traits in common with his mother, but that he repudiated these traits as evidences of weakness and femininity, and in so doing repudiated her.

(k) Rejection of Mother

To the extent that Hitler respected and emulated his father, he disrespected and denied his mother. Some evidence to demonstrate this point will be brought forward in a later section. Hitler probably loved his mother very much as a person, but his strong dependent attachment to her was a humiliating sign of his incapacity to take care of himself, and hence he was forced to belittle the relationship. At eighteen years he was too near to her weakness, not feminine enough and yet not male enough, to respect her. He writes:

(i) I owe much to the time in which I had learned to become hard (in Vienna)… I praise it even more for having rescued me from the emptiness of an easy life (in Linz with his mother), that it took the milksop out of his downy nest and gave him Dame Sorrow for a foster mother…(M.K. 29).

Hanisch reports that in Vienna, Hitler manifested a queer idealism about love;" but had very little respect for the female sex. Every woman, he believed, could be bad. This remark falls in with the evidence to be presented later which suggests that, for a time, Adolf was indignant with his mother for submitting to his father, and in the end scorned her for so doing. Since he has always been contemptuous of physical weakness, one might expect him to be contemptuous of women, and there are some facts to show that this is true. It is even possible that after Herr Hitler's death, the adolescent Adolf, adopting his father's role to some extent, sometimes lashed his mother with insolent words and maybe struck her. If this were true, it would help explain his exceeding grief on the occasion of her death - guilt contributing to his dejection - and it might explain a striking passage in MEIN KAMPF in which Hitler describes the typical lower class family.

(i) When, at the age of fourteen, the young lad is dismissed from school (Adolf dropped school when he was about sixteen years), it is difficult to say which is worse; his unbelievable ignorance as far as knowledge and ability are concerned, or the biting impudence of his behavior combined with an immorality which makes one's hair stand on end, considering his age (Adolf's immorality came to the notice of his teachers at the age of twelve years)… The three year-old child has now become a youth of fifteen who despises all authority; (recall Adolf's conflict with his father)...

Now he loiters about, and God only knows when he comes home. (See p. 7…"caused my mother much grief, made me anything but a stay-at-home"). For a change he may even "beat the poor creature who

was once his mother, curses God and the world"...
(M.K. 43-44).

(L) Evidence will be advanced later to show that
one of the most potent impressions of Hitler's
early life was that of <u>a relationship in which a
domineering and severe old man (his father) bullied
and scornfully maltreated a gentle and compliant
woman (his mother).</u> The effects of being reared
under these conditions were lasting; the experience
made it impossible for him to believe in, hope for,
or enjoy a relationship marked by peace, love and
tenderness.

(m) The outstanding press of the boy's early life
were those of <u>p - Aggression</u> and <u>p – Rejection.</u>
The former came mostly from his father, the latter
from many people. Among the specific causes of
this idea of having been rejected we would list (1)
the birth of a younger sister, Paula, in 1895 or 1896;
(2) the opposition of his father; (3) his repeated
failures at school; (4) his lack of friends; (5) the
death of both parents, making It necessary for him,
a penniless, uneducated and unemployed orphan, to
face the world alone. The sense of being rejected by
his family is in many passages expressed in
connection with his feeling of being excluded from
membership in the German nation. This point will
be taken up later.

(i) Are we not the same as all the other Germans? Do we not all belong together? This problem now began to whirl through my little head for the first time. After cautious questioning, I heard with envy the reply that not every German was fortunate enough to belong to Bismarck's Reich. This I could not understand. (M.K. 9).

(ii) An unnatural separation from the great common Motherland* (M.N.O. 469).

(n) <u>Repudiation of Past Self and Family Connections.</u>

Knowing Hitler's fanatical sentiments against mixed marriages, impure blood, the lower classes and the Jewish race, it is important to note the following facts:

(i) His forebears come from a region in which the blood of Bavarians, Bohemians, Moravians, Czechs and Slovakians have mixed for generations. Without doubt all of these strains are represented in him.

(ii) His father was illegitimate; his grandfather may have been a Viennese Jew.

(iii) His godfather, Herr Prinz, was a Viennese Jew.

(iv) His father had three wives; one a waitress, one a domestic servant, and a number of women on the side (hearsay).

(v) His father begot at least one child out of marriage.

(vi) Klara Poelzl, his mother, was Alois Hitler's second cousin once removed and also his ward (twenty-three years younger). Special permission from the Church had to be obtained before he could marry her.

(vii) Angela Hitler, Adolf's older half-sister, ran a restaurant for Jewish students In Vienna.

(viii) Paula Hitler, Adolf 's younger sister, was the mistress of a Viennese Jew for a while.

(ix) A cousin of Hitler's is feeble-minded; most of the other members of his clan are ignorant, illiterate or mentally retarded. He himself had to repeat the first year of Realschule (Technical High School) and failed to graduate.

Thus, Hitler has spent a good part of his life cursing and condemning people who belong to his layer of society, who resemble members of his own clan;

who have characteristics similar to his own. On the other hand, the ideal he has set up, the person he pretends to be, is the exact opposite of all this. We have a fairly clear case, then, of <u>Counteraction</u> against inferiority feelings and self-contempt. Between 1903, when he left, and 1958, after the Anschluss, Hitler never visited his home and never communicated with his relatives (except in the case of his half- sister Angela). Unlike Napoleon, he did not carry his family along with him as he ascended to the heights of power. In this we see a Rejection of his past self and family connections.

(o) <u>Identification with Germany</u>.

Hitler's egocentrism has always been so marked, he has been such a Bohemian, (if not a lone wolf in many phases of his career) that his undoubted devotion to Germany strikes one as most unusual. Since this devotion began at an early age and was the factor, more than any other, which decided that he would become a supreme success rather than an utter failure, it is worthwhile noting here the forces, so far mentioned, which brought about this intense insociation:

(i) Influence of Ludwig Poetsch, his teacher, who, serving as a substitute father, glorified the history of

Germany and presented Bismarck's Reich as an ideal.

(ii) Influence of a strong nationalist association among Hitler's classmates.

(iii) Cathexis of power. The figures of Frederick the Great, Bismarck and others offered better foci of admiration than did Austrian heroes.

(iv) Insociation with a more powerful nation satisfied his youthful pride, raised his status in his own eyes and allowed him to reject his inferior, Austrian self.

(v) Heightened cathexis of an object behind a barrier. This is a general principle: that an individual will idealize an object that he cannot quite attain - so near yet so far. In this connection, it is interesting to note that the great majority of dictators have not been natives of the country that they came to dominate. Hitler's continued sympathy for Germans outside the Reich is evidently a projection of his own self-pity as an Ostmarkian.

(v-1) (Memel returns to the Reich) I thereby lead you back into that home which you have not forgotten and which has never forgotten you. (M.1T.0. 614).

(vi) Displacement of defiance against the father. By identifying himself with Germany, the boy Adolf found an object even greater than his stern father, which permitted him to give vent to his frustrated rebelliousness against his Austrian parent.

(vii) Germany as a substitute mother. In view of the press rejection suffered in childhood, it is likely - and much evidence for this hypothesis will be presented later - that Germany represented a kind of foster parent. It is even possible that Hitler, as a child, entertained a foster parent fantasy.

He speaks of being Bavarian by blood, a statement- for which there is no known justification. This point will be fully discussed later in describing his devotions to Germany's cause in 1918, the hour of her deepest humiliation. In many places Hitler speaks of Germany in words that one might use In speaking of a beloved woman.

(vii-1) ...the longing grew stronger to go there (Germany) where, since my early youth, I had been drawn by secret wishes and secret love. (M.K. 16I).

(vii-2) What I first bad looked upon as an impassable chasm now spurred me on to a greater love for my country than ever before. (M.K. 55).

(vii-3) Heiden, quoting from Hitler: The hundreds of thousands who love their country more than anything else must also be loved by their country more than anything else.

(vii-4) I appeal to those who, severed from the motherland, have to fight for the holy treasure of their language...find who now in painful emotion long for the hour that will allow them to return to the arms of the beloved mother. (M.K. 161).

The common expression for Germans is Fatherland, but Hitler very often substitutes Motherland, He speaks of "the common motherland," the great German motherland," "the German mother of all life." This is not unnatural since he, once a very dependent adolescent, was left penniless and un-befriended after the death of his mother. We are not surprised, therefore, to find him speaking of being removed "from the emptiness of an easy life, that it took the milksop out of his downy nest and gave him Dame Sorrow for a foster mother," and speaking also of the time "when the Goddess of Misery took me into her arms." It is reported that he was mothered by several older ladies in his early Munich days and seemed to find comfort in such relationships. In 1920, for example, he found a sort of home with Frau Hoffman. He always had to send her, according to Holden, his latest portrait, on which he would write, for example: "*To my dear, faithful little Mother, Christmas 1925, from her respectful Adolf Hitler.*"

B. VIENNA DAYS: 1908 – 1913

The chief facts pertinent to the present analysis are these:

1. Klara Hitler was operated on for cancer of the breast in the early summer of 1907. On December 21, 1907, she died. Two months before her death, Adolf Hitler went to Vienna and was examined by the Academy School of Art. He failed. He moved to. Vienna in the winter of 1908, and the following October presented himself again at the Academy. But the drawings he brought as illustrations of his work were considered so lacking in talent that he was not allowed to take the examination. He was told he would make a better architect than painter, though he himself reports that he was a better colorist than draftsman.

2. Some account of these years has been given us by Hanisch, a "bum" from Bohemia who befriended him. They were fellow members of the same hostel, or flophouse. The first thing Hitler said to Hanisch sounds like a projection of **(1)** press Rejection and **(2)** press Aggression. He said **(1)** his landlady had dispossessed him and now he was without shelter, and **(2)** he had begged a drunken man for a few pennies but the latter had raised his cane and insulted him. Hitler was very bitter about this.

3. Hitler wore a beard during this period and in his long overcoat looked very much like a certain type of Oriental Jew not uncommon in Vienna. Hitler had a number of Jewish acquaintances and sold postcards that he painted to Jewish dealers. There was no evidence during these first years of any hostility to Jews. Only later, after he had listened excitedly to the speeches of the anti-Semitic mayor, Lueger, did he become an avowed, and somewhat later a fanatical, Anti-Semite himself.

4. Hitler was exceedingly lazy and procrastinating in doing so little water colors during these days. He was much more interested in haranguing the other inmates of the hostel on the subject of politics Already he had vague notions of founding a party.

5. He devoted some time to thinking up little devices for making money through trickery. According to one informant, his name is in the Vienna police records as having been accused of theft, and it is suggested that his departure for

Munich in 1913 was prompted by a desire to avoid serving a term in jail.

6. Hitler's friendship with Hanisch came to an abrupt end when he accused the latter of stealing money from him. This has the flavor of a typical Hitlerian projection.

7. Hanisch reports that Hitler's love for Germany and his hate for Austria were vociferously expressed on all occasions during these years.

8. Hitler was shocked by what he saw of sexual practices in Vienna. Hanisch speaks of his having a purity complex.

9. According to one informant, Hitler is down in the police records of Vienna as a sex pervert.

10. In 1913, Hitler left Vienna and entered the country of which he had long yearned to be a citizen. He became a resident of Munich.

11. The press of Rejection is perhaps the outstanding feature of the Vienna period. There was, in the first place, the rejection by the Academy of Arts, which Hitler felt was based on his inadequate education. This left a resentment against intellectuals generally, which was never stilled. The following excerpt sums up his conclusions on this point.

(i) Generally, it is the children of higher place, momentarily well-to-do parents who, in turn, are deemed worthy of a higher education. Hereby questions of talent play a subordinate role.

Many Other passages speak eloquently of insults to his pride received at the hands of the privileged world of the gay capital.

(i) …the graciously patronizing attitudes of a certain part of the fashionable world (both in skirts and. trousers) whose 'sympathy for the people' is at times as haughty as it is obtrusive and tactless.

(ii) Vienna, the city that to so many represents the idea of harmless gaiety - the festive place for merrymaking - is to me the only living memory of the most miserable time of my life.

12. Hitler spent five years in Vienna. Living as he was, penniless among the penniless of the lower class, he himself experienced, and he was in close touch with others, who experienced the basic wants and viewpoints of the depressed victims of civilization. Here, certainly, was much food for thought. He also attended sessions of parliament and numerous political mass meetings, and observed the proceedings critically. From the start, he was constantly preoccupied with the question; why does this political movement fail and that one succeed? It was natural for him to think realistically and strategically; not to make the common mistake of supposing man to be better than he is, and yet taking full account of his heroic potentialities, having observed that millions of simple untutored men will gladly fight and sacrifice their lives for an ideal vividly presented. In addition; Hitler spent many hours in the public library looking over histories and books dealing with social questions. MEIN KAMPF proves that the young man from Linz who could not get through High School was capable of profiting by what he saw and read, and that these five years of drifting and irregular employment were by no means wasted. The flophouse and the beer hall were his Heidelberg and University of Vienna. He writes:

(i) So in a few years I built a foundation of knowledge from which I still draw nourishment today. (M.K. 29).

(ii) At that time I formed an image of the world and a view of life which became the granite foundation for my actions. (M.K. 30).

13. For the Vienna period the critical question psychologically is this: why did Hitler, living among the proletariat, find the developed ideology of communism repellent and the embryonic ideology of fascism appealing? The chief determinants of his choice, as they occur to me, are these:

(i) Hitler's father belonged to the lower middle class. Having moved one rung up the ladder by years of effort, his pride compelled him to draw a sharp line between himself and those below him. No one has stated this principle of behavior better than his son:

(i-1) The reason for that which one could almost call hostility is the fact that a social class, which has only recently worked its way up from the level of manual labor, fears to fall back into the old, but little esteemed, class, or at least fears being counted in with that class. In addition, many remember with disgust the misery existing in the lower class; the frequent brutality of their daily social contacts; their own position in society, however small it may be, makes every contact with the state of life and culture, which they in turn have left behind, unbearable.

This explains why members of the higher social

class can frequently lower themselves to the humblest of their fellow beings with less embarrassment than seems possible to the 'upstarts'. For an upstart is anyone who, through his own energy, works his way up from his previous social position to a higher one.

Finally, <u>this relentless struggle kills all pity</u>. One's own painful scramble for existence suffocates the feeling of sympathy for the misery of those left behind. (M.K. 31-32).

Brought up by such a father, it was natural for Adolf Hitler to envy and admire his social superiors and to look with contempt upon those of a lower station. As the American editors of MEIN KAMPF have put it;

(ii) Hitler, conscious of belonging to a higher social caste than his fellow workers…instinctively retreats from the idea of accepting solidarity with them. (M.K. 56).

(iii) Hitler had already been identified for some years with the German Nationalist movement and so his unit of insociation (group identification and belongingness) was greatly threatened by the communists' unit of insociation, the manual workers of the world. The former would lead logically to a war between nations, the latter to a war between classes. Communism was the greatest enemy of nationalism.

(iv) Parallel to his naturalistic sentiments was Hitler's enthusiasm for the military, a professional class which is antipathetic to communists generally. The former finds its goal in Power and Glory, the latter in Peace and Prosperity.

(v) Hitler had great reverence for the strong and contempt for the weak and therefore favored a stratified social system; a dictatorship of the elite. There was no compassion in his makeup; he had little sympathy for the under-dog. His ideology was founded on the rise to power of nature's supermen involving relationships of dominance and sub-mission among men. Communism was founded on the notion of equality.

C. WAR EXPERIENCES 1914 – 1919

The record of these years is conflicting, but the following points are probably true and pertinent to our theme.

1. In enlisting in the Army, Hitler became incorporated for the first time. Never before had he been an accepted member of a respected institution.

This was not only a great relief to him, enabling him to forget the long series of past failures, but it provided a ground for pride and a sense of security. At last, he and the German nation were one.

2. There is no evidence that Hitler was ever in a front line trench. It seems that he served as a messenger and was required to traverse ground that was being shelled by the enemy. Hitler, it appears, was quick to offer himself for dangerous tasks of this kind and was said to be an adept at running and then falling or seeking shelter behind some obstacle when the fire became intense. In this he showed courage. There is no record, however, in the War Department of any episode such as has been described in connection with his winning the Iron Cross, First Order, Apparently he was awarded this medal after he had left the Front, supposedly gassed in one of the last offensives of the Allies.

3. Informants have commented on Hitler's marked subservience to the superior officers, offering to do their washing and perform other menial tasks, courting their good graces to such an extent that his comrades were disgusted.

4. Hitler was the only man in his company to never receive any mail or packages from home, and at Christmas and other occasions when the others were receiving gifts and messages he sulked moodily by himself. Here is another instance of press rejection.

5. It is hard to explain the fact that in four years of service he was not promoted above the rank of corporal. The comment by one of his officers that he was a neurotic fellow is the only explanation that has been advanced.

6. It seems certain that Hitler was not gassed to any serious extent in 1918, but that he suffered from a war neurosis - hysterical blindness - which also deprived him of his voice and perhaps his hearing. This psychosomatic illness was concomitant with the final defeat of his Mother Germany, and it was after hearing the news of her capitulation that he had his vision of his task.as savior. Suddenly his sight was restored.

7. In 1918, Hitler the soldier became very disturbed at the surprising success of Allied propaganda and then there occurred a reaction that was typical of his whole character, namely, to admire and then to acquire the technique of a powerful opponent.

Hitler with fellow patients at Pasewalk, 1918

(i) We had a chance to become acquainted with the incredible disciplines of our opponents' propaganda, and still today it is my pride to have found the means for beating, finally, its very makers. Two years later I was master of this craft.

D. POST-WAR HISTORY: 1919

From 1919 to the present, Hitler's doings are less obscure then for the periods so far reviewed. A great many of the facts are a matter of common knowledge and we will not review them in this section. A few points, however, are worthy of being highlighted.

1. For a year or two after his release from the military hospital, Hitler was more or less footloose, "a stray dog looking for a master," according to one informant. Undoubtedly, there were more instances of press-rejection to embitter him.

2. He was still a member of the Reichswehr, when his superior officer, discovering his ability for public speaking, assigned him the task of indoctrinating the soldiers with the desired ideology. Later he was asked to speak to a civilian group. This success encouraged him to go further and to enter politics for life. Hitler's realization that he had the power to sway large masses of people was the second crucial factor, next to his revelation in the hospital while blind, in determining his career. His phenomenal success hinged on his mass-rousing talent.

3. After hearing Fedar speak, Hitler was prompted to join a small group that called itself the National Socialist Workers Party. Within a year he was its moving spirit and sole leader, and it might fairly be said that he was its creator as it now exists - the difference between its status before he joined and soon afterwards being so great.

No doubt Hitler had been making speeches in

fantasy since his boyhood and had done a good deal of informal haranguing throughout this whole period; first as the adolescent ringleader of the young Nationalists at school; second as a ham politician among the derelicts of the Vienna slums; and third as a corporal behind the lines; but his sudden emergence as a spiritual force during the period 1921 - 1923 brought him into a much magnified sphere of activity which was qualitatively different. A selection from MEIN KAMPF, which is unquestionably autobiographical in reference, might be quoted here as a hint of how the transformation was apperceived by him:

In the monotony of everyday life, even important people often seem unimportant, and they hardly stand out over the average of their surroundings; but as soon as they are faced by a situation in which others would despair or go wrong, out of' the plain average child the ingenious nature grows visibly, not infrequently to the astonishment of all those who hitherto had an opportunity to observe him, who had meanwhile grown up in the smallness of bourgeois life, and therefore, in consequence of this process, the prophet has rarely any honor in his own country. Never is there a better opportunity to observe this than during war. In the hours of distress, when others despair, out of apparently harmless children there shoot, suddenly, heroes of death-defying determination and icy coolness of reflection.

If this hour of trial had never come, then hardly anyone would ever have been able to guess that a young hero is hidden in the beardless boy. Nearly always such an impetus is needed in order to call genius into action. Fate's hammer stroke, which then throws that one to the ground, suddenly strikes steel in another, and while now the shell of everyday life is broken, the erstwhile nucleus lies open to the eyes of the astonished world. (M.K. 402-3).

4. It seems clear that it was (1) the defeat of Germany and (2) the opposition against which he had to strive that acted as instigators to his behavior from then on, which became more and more aggressively dominant. The idea of being a revolutionary was a necessary impetus to action:

"We National Socialists know that with this opinion we stand as revolutionaries in the world of today, and that we are branded as s such. But our thinking and acting must not be determined by the applause or the rejection of our time." (M.K.595-6).

5. Hitler was chiefly attracted during these early years to a homosexual, Ernst Roehm, a superior officer with an upper class background. The physical strength and social assurance of Roehm were much envied, and, to have the political backing of such a figure gave Hitler a sense of security.

6. Up to the famous Munich Putsch, (1923), Hitler was conspicuous in his worship of and flattering subservience to ranking officers in the Amy, especially in these days in his relations with General Ludendorff; but from 1924 on, although he never entirely lost a certain embarrassment in the presence of his former superiors, there was a change from abasement to dominance, and even arrogance, in dealing with aristocrats and war lords.

7. The chief points in his political program were these:

(a) Wiping the Versailles Treaty off the books.
(b) Denial of war guilt.
(c) Resurrection of Germany as a military power of the first order.
(d) Militaristic expansion dominated by the motive of revenge against the Allies, and
(e) Anti-Semitism - soon afterwards
(f) The purification of the German people by a variety of hygienic measures was added as an essential aim or policy.

8. During the years from 1923 to 1933, Hitler's emotional outbursts; his tantrums of rage and indignation; his spells of weeping and threats of self-annihilation increased in frequency and intensity.

This can be partly accounted for by the fact that they were effective in bringing his associates around to his point of view. Instead of antagonizing the group of revolutionaries who, with him were plotting to usurp power, these frightful orgies of passion served to intimidate them. Everyone sought to avoid topics that would bring about the fits.

9. Among the reasons given in extenuation of the cold-blooded purge of 1934 were (a) that the victims were disgusting homosexuals and (b) that they were plotting to snatch power and supersede him.

10. During the last twenty years, rumors have periodically arisen and spread to the effect that Hitler was enamored of this or that young woman; most of these were either fabricated for one reason or another or premature, since the appeal that certain women, of the stage, particularly, had for Hitler was generally short-lived. The one affair that stands out is that with a nineteen-year-old Angela (Geli) Raubal, his niece. Hitler was often in her company and was pathologically jealous of any attentions shown her by other men. Two informants have stated positively that Hitler murdered the girl, but the official report was suicide. Whichever story is correct, however, we gain the impression of a peculiar and stormy relationship. Rumors have it that Hitler's sexual life, such as it is, demands a unique performance on the part of the women, the exact nature of which is a state secret.

11. A great deal has been made in Germany of Hitler's asceticism, but this, when you come down to it, amounts to a vegetarian diet, served to him by the best chef in the Reich, and a great variety of soft drinks in place of hard liquor. It is said that he did not permanently give up meat until after the death of his niece, Geli.

V. PERSONALITY STRUCTURE

A. EGO, SUPEREGO AND ID

1. Ego

According to the criteria we are accustomed to use in measuring ego strength and structure, Hitler's ego is surprisingly weak. Here we are of course using the term ego to apply to an institution of the personality (not to narcissism or self-esteem). Hitler is conspicuously low in the following powers:

(a) <u>Deficient ability to organize and coordinate his efforts.</u>

(i) During his boyhood, especially at the time he was living as an indulged youngster in his mother's apartment, Hitler's activities were markedly irregular and aimless. He was unable to apply himself except when his impulse prompted him to do so.

(ii) Hanisch reports that in Vienna, Hitler was never an ardent worker; was unable to get up in the morning; had difficulty in getting started; suffered from paralysis of the will. He always stopped work the moment he had earned a little money, explaining that, "he must have some leisure, he was not a coolie".

(iii) According to Rauschning, "He does not know how to work steadily. Indeed, he is incapable of working. He gets ideas, impulses, the realization of which must be feverishly achieved and immediately gotten rid of. He does not know what it is to work continuously. Everything about him is "spasm," to use a favorite word of his.

(iv) Although Hitler prescribes disciplined order of work for those about him, he himself lives like an artist or Bohemian. His habits are as erratic and irregular as his temper. He may go to bed at eleven or four a.m., getting up at seven or at noon. He is rarely punctual.

(v) According to Rauschning again; "Hitler seems a man of tremendous will power, but the appearance is deceptive. He is languid and apathetic by nature and needs the stimulus of nervous excitement to rouse him out of chronic lethargy into spasmodic activity.

(b) <u>Deficient ability to resolve conflicts.</u>

Hitler has always suffered from periods of indecisiveness and mental confusion that incapacitate him to the extent of being unable to make any decision or come to any conclusion. Then, quite suddenly, his inner voice will speak, but as a rule, not until the situation has become threatening. As Roehm says, "Usually he solves suddenly, at the very last moment…only because he vacillates and procrastinates."

(c) <u>Deficient ability to control emotion.</u>

His tantrums have been often described, and even

though it be admitted that Hitler has a capacity to turn them on and off as he sees fit, still, such unmanly display of infantile intolerance to frustration, of tears and shrieks, is entirely out of keeping with his own ideal of the Iron Supermensch.

(i) Rauschning: "My own experience of him, and what I have learned from others, indicates a lack of control amounting to total demoralization."

(d) <u>Deficient objectivity.</u>

Distortion of human behavior and social events by frequent projections giving rise to delusions of all sorts.

(e) <u>Disjunctivity of thought and speech.</u>

All of Hitler's writings and reported speeches exhibit a disorganization of ideas and verbal-expression which at times verge's on the pathological.

(f) <u>Insight deficiency.</u>

Hitler has never shown any capacity to perceive or admit his errors and defects. Part of this is a conscious determination to follow the policy of denying them, this being considered by him politically expedient.

(g) <u>Inability to keep his word and fulfill obligations.</u>

(i) It has been said that "Hitler discards with perfect ease everything that a moment before has passed as a fixed principle. His political attitude is characterized by two things: first, an unbelievable capacity to tell falsehood, and second, a quite disarming naiveté, a total innocence of promises and assertions made only a moment before."

(h) <u>In contrast to these signs of weakness, Hitler is high - sometimes very high - on the following criteria:</u>

(i) Power to do what he wants to do and has the capacity to do.

(ii) Counteractive re-striving.

(iii) Power to resist undesirable coercions from society.

(iv) Power to resist dictatorship of conventional superego.

(v) Initiative and self-sufficiency.

(vi) Ability to take responsibility and effectively direct others.

(vii) Long apperceptive span (taking account of a distant future in making decisions).

(i) The situation may be briefly formulated by stating that <u>Hitler operates on thalamic energy rather than on conscious will and rational planning.</u> Possessed by fanatical passion he can accomplish things which those who act on cooler and more moderate plans fall to achieve. The force, in other words, comes from the id, and the ego is used in its service. This combination is typical of the gangster; but Hitler is different from the ordinary type, hawing some of the attributes of the romantic artist. He la a compound, say, of Lord Byron and A1 Capone.

2. Id

Under the term id, I am including all unconscious psychic processes -- principally affective and conative processes which emerge suddenly without voluntary effort and take possession of the ego, but also unconscious Intellective processes resulting in sudden judgments and decisions. Such processes are an important part of every man's psychology. It.is only when they play an unusually dominant role in determining action that we stress them. They are especially prominent in the intuitive type. Hitler being, one of these, Hitler's sentiments in this regard conform to his behavior.

(i) We must distrust the intelligence and the conscience and must place our trust in our instincts.

We have to regain a new simplicity. (Quoted by Rauschning).

(ii) Over-educated people, stuffed with knowledge and intellect, but bare of any sound instincts...

(iii) ...Of secondary importance is the training of mental abilities. (M.K. 613).

Hitler's basic assumption, as Max Lerner points out, is that there are no logical categories in the perception of values but only an intuitionism that is its own principle and its own justification. He functions, in other words, as does a creative artist, which is unusual in one who chooses politics as his field. It is his dependence on involuntary processes that gives rise to his inability to make decisions about a hundred and one little matters that come to him in the routine of his daily occupation. He must wait upon the spirit.

(iv) In the subconscious, the work goes on. It matures, sometimes it dies. Unless I have the inner incorruptible conviction: this is the solution. I do nothing. Not even if the whole party tried to drive me to action. I will not act; I will wait, no matter what happens. But if the voice speaks then I know the time has some to act. (Quoted from Rauschning).

Many acquaintances have remarked on Hitler's periods of abstraction and revery. He "spent his time building castles in the air," Hanisch reports. "I had the impression," writes Rauschning, "that he was not listening, his thoughts were far away." Another informant, Roberts, believes that Hitler, wrapped up in his dream world, is unaware of a large part of the practical activities and even brutalities of his party. His movements would be impossible without the continued cooperation of men like Goebbels, Goering and Himmler. Because of the tremendous downward pull of unconscious processes, Hitler must often pull himself up by the bootstraps, as it were, to meet an emergency.

(v) I go my way with the certainty and security of a somnambulist.

Among id processes, we should stress particularly that dynamic pattern of energy bolted up in him which we call the unity and orienting themas. This compound of motivations, which amounts to a monomaniacal idea, will be fully described later. It is a rigid, fanatical and incurable reservoir of the thalamic energies which, on release, have two or three times the potency that a normal man brings to bear upon any one reasonable object. The ego is in collaboration with this unconscious complex, operates in its service and can, within limits, call it into play or check it momentarily. On appropriate occasions, indeed, Hitler makes good use of his capacity to be possessed by the complex. He dramatizes it, whips it up, and, intoxicated by the words that pour out of his mouth, deliriously gives vent to his passion.

Also characteristic of one who so readily acquiesces to the demi-urge is Hitler's superstitiousness, his feeling that he is an object of divine protection, his tendency to interpret striking events as signs or omens of success or failure. Like many a religious leader he is said to hear voices and see spirits. Here we would compare him to Joseph Smith, the founder of Mormonism, the chief difference being that Smith's voices gave him permission to free the sex instinct, whereas Hitler's voices encourage brutality and destruction. Hitler also bears comparison to Mary Baker Eddy.

1. Hysteroid Personality.

It is clear from what has been said that Hitler has manifested many features of the hysteroid type of make-up. Besides the definitely recorded hysterical attack of blindness and aphonia (in 1918), there are his paroxysms of emotion; his hallucinations coming out of nightmares; his sudden revelations and hearing of inner voices, and the periods of daydreaming and abstraction, all of which are reminiscent of hysterics, inspired and uninspired, of which the history of religion furnishes so many striking examples. Here he might be likened, perhaps, to Joan of Arc.

2. Schizophrenic Features.

It will be made clear as we go on that Hitler is possessed by a complete semi-delusional system characteristic of paranoid schizophrenia. Beside this, many of the symptoms which have been listed in the previous paragraph tinder hysteroid personality are also typical of schizoid states. The enormous banked-up hate and revengefulness in the man, and the acts of cruelty which he is able to execute, apparently without the normal recriminations of conscience are also symptomatic of schizophrenia.

Although it might be said that Hitler is an hysteric on the verge of schizophrenia, and this may be truer today than it was a while ago, still it must be acknowledged that conditions in Germany have been such, and the man's success in imposing his delusional system on his fellow countrymen has been so phenomenal, that he has remained within the boundaries of technical sanity.

3. Superego.

It seems clear that Hitler is not an amoral brute like Goering or the majority of his followers; that is to say, his close followers. He has a superego but it is repressed, the mechanisms of the ego being set up against its interference. The conditions that usually prevail might be described as an alliance between the ego and the instinctual forces of the id against the dictates of the superego. A great deal of endo-psychic energy is wrapped up in this effort to repress and deny the superego and the guilt feelings that it gives rise to. Its activity, however, can be judged by (1) the vehemence of his affirmations of brutality (and thus his denial of conscience); (2) the justifications that he feels called upon to give when his actions are particularly repellant to the con-science of his world, and; (3) certain symptoms that are generally recognizable as indications of unconscious superego activity.

Surely Hitler is speaking of himself as well as of others when he writes:

(i) Only when the time comes when the race is no longer overshadowed by the consciousness of its own guilt, then it will find internal peace and external energy to cut down, regardless-ly and brutally, the wild shoots, and to pull up the weeds.

That Hitler sees himself as the destroyer of an antiquated Hebraic Christian superego is shown by many passages:

(ii) I am freeing men from the restraints of an intelligence that has taken charge; from the dirty and degrading modifications of a chimera called conscience and morality, and from the demands of a freedom and personal independence which only a very few can bear.

(iii) We must be ruthless. We must regain our clear conscience as to ruthlessness. Only thus shall we purge our people of their softness and sentimental Philistinism, and their degenerate delight in beer-swilling.

(iv) I recognize no moral law in politics.

(v) Conscience is a Jewish invention. It is a blemish like circumcision.

Obviously, Hitler is posing here as the Nietzschean Anti-Christ who is going to create a new superego for mankind; the exact antithesis of that which has prevailed since the establishment of Christianity. This pose, however, is for the benefit of his close followers such as Rauschning, who has recorded the above assertions. "Moral commonplaces," he affirms, "are indispensable for the masses. Nothing is more mistaken than for a politician to pose as a non-moral superman." The tenor of many of Hitler's public speeches, however, prove that he has not entirely conquered his superego, acquired during early years under the influence of his pious mother, the Catholic monastery at Lambach and his teachers at school. 'The following may be taken as examples of an unquiet conscience:

(vi) It (Storm Troop) did not want to establish violence as its aim, but it wanted to protect the messengers of the spiritual aim against oppression by violence. (M.K. 79O).

(vii) However, I did not wish to carry out my purposes by force. Instead, I did my utmost to accomplish my purpose by persuasion alone.

(viii) It never has been my intention to wage wars, but rather to build… (M.N.O. 836).

(ix) I forbade the sacrifice of more human lives than was absolutely necessary. (Speaking of the war with Poland. M.N.O. 723).

There is.no question that Hitler succeeds in repressing his superego most of the time. He has consciously and openly committed most of the crimes on the calendar, so much so that the diagnosis "psychopathic personality" or "moral imbecile" seems almost justified; however, there are many indications that a superego of sorts operates unconsciously. After the bloody purge of 1934, for example, it is said that he was not able to sleep quietly for weeks. At night, he prowled restlessly up and down. His expressions and fearful nightmares can be explained in part as resultants of disquieting guilt feelings. Also to be included in this category are his frequent thoughts of suicide. These are often avowed, to be sure, with the purpose of impressing his close followers; but they are also in conformity with an unconscious tendency. According to our hypothesis, in fact, we would attribute a good many of Hitler's later acts of aggression to his superego. They are crimes to appease conscience. <u>Having once started on a career of brutality, he can only quiet the pain of a bed conscience by going on with ever greater ruthlessness to achieve successes, and so to demonstrate to himself and others that God approves of him and his methods.</u> This dynamism, however, can work only in so far as his aggressions are successful; that is, only good fortune can prove that conscience (anticipatory anxiety) was wrong -- there was nothing to be afraid of after all. Failure will undoubtedly be followed by guilt feelings. Further evidences of superego activity can be found in the character of the projections so common in

Hitler's speeches and writings, as we shall now show.

4. <u>Ego Defense Mechanisms: Projection</u>.

By far the most common form of defense mechanism in Hitler's personality is that of projection. This works in the service of self-esteem, in blinding him both to his guiltiness and to his inferiority. There is no record of any case in which this process is used so often and so intensely. It operates so promptly and consistently, indeed, that by paying close attention to the objects that Hitler scorns and condemns one gets a fairly accurate and comprehensive view of his own id. His case is rather unusual in that he has consciously adopted and furthered what was once no doubt a purely unconscious mechanism. For example, he says, "As soon as by one's own propaganda even a glimpse of right on the other side is admitted, the cause for doubting of one's own right is laid." The necessary corollary to this proposition would be: as soon as one's own wrong is admitted, the cause for doubting the wrong of one's opponent is laid. He also has enough knowledge to realize that accusations are evidences of guilt, for, he says, "If they now say that this is the signal that Germany now wants to attack the entire world, I do not believe that this is meant seriously: such could only be the expression of a bad conscience." -- a remarkable statement to be made by the world's greatest projector.

Two or three illustrations would suffice to make plain the nature of Hitler's projections, but they represent such unique descriptions of himself that a larger collection of examples will be of interest to psychologists.

(i) In Vienna, Hanisch tells us, Hitler wore a long coat given him by a Jewish friend, "an incredibly greasy derby on the back of his head. His hair was long and tangled and he grew a beard on his chin such as we Christians seldom have, though one is not uncommon in...the Jewish ghettos...Hitler at that time looked very Jewish, so that I often joked with him that he must be of Jewish blood, since such a large beard rarely grows on a Christian's chin."

Compare this to Hitler's account of the first conspicuously Jewish person he met in Vienna. "I suddenly came upon a being clad in a long caftan, with black curls. Is this also a Jew?, was my first thought." Then he goes on to list the repellent traits of the Jew: "Later the smell of these caftan wearers often made me ill. Added to this was their dirty clothes and their none-too-heroic appearance. Recalling Hitler's immorality at school and the fact that he is down (according to one informant) in the

Vienna police records as a sex pervert, the following statement is pertinent:

"Aside from the physical uncleanliness, it was repelling, suddenly, to discover the perioral blemishes of the chosen people."

(ii) Hitler was charged with theft In Vienna, according to one informant, and yet Hitler broke off his friendship with Hanish by wrongfully accusing him of having misappropriated a water color of his worth fifty Kronen.

(iii) In daily life Hitler oscillates between extreme energy and utter listlessness, and yet Hitler: "All passivity, all inertia, is senseless, inimical to life."

(iv) Hitler has never admitted to being wrong. According to the Nazi creed, Hitler is always right, and yet -- Hitler: "These Impudent rascals (intellectuals) who always know everything better than anybody else…"

"The intellect has grown autocratic, and has become a disease of life."

(v) Hitler has often affirmed that he was governed by instinct and intuition rather than by reason.

Hitler: "The people…are so feminine in their nature and attitude that their activities and thoughts are motivated less by sober considerations than by feeling and sentiment.

(vi) Roehm has said: "He doesn't even seem to be aware how dishonest he is." By now the whole world agrees that Hitler is a monumental liar."

Hitler: "What a race (Jews): As such they have been nailed down forever…the great masters of lying."

(vii) Hitler has a way of staring at people as if he were attempting to hypnotize them.

Hitler: "They...tried to pierce me even with their eyes. Innumerable faces were turned toward me with sullen hatred."

(viii) Hitler's favorite entertainment is to witness private performances of naked, dancing.

Hitler; "Chicherin, and with him a staff of over two hundred Soviet Jews --visits the cabarets, watches naked dancers perform for his pleasure…"

(ix) Below I have listed a miscellany of Hitler's

statements which are more accurate as descriptions of himself than they are of others.

a. In such hours I had sad forebodings and was filled with a depressing, fear. I was faced by a doctrine (Social Democrats) consisting of egoism and hatred; it could be victorious, following mathematical laws, but at the same time it could bring about the end of mankind.

b. Social Democracy…directs a bombardment of lies and calumnies towards the adversary who seemed most dangerous, till finally the nerves of those who had been attacked give out and they, for the sake of peace, bow down to the hated enemy.

c. They (opponents at Nazi meetings) resembled a powder keg that might blow up at any moment, and to which the burning fuse has been attached.

d. For his (the Jew's) entire activity is unrestricted by moral obligations.

e. I talked until my tongue was weary and till my throat was hoarse…of the destructiveness of their Marxist doctrine of irrationality.

f. …we will not let the Jews slit our gullets and not defend ourselves.

g. (Jew)…the higher he climbs, the more alluringly rises out of the veil of the past, his old goal, once promised to him, and with feverish greed he watches in his brightest heads the dream of world domination step into tangible proximity.

h. They (Marxists) began to treat us as genuine chief criminals of humanity.

i. For this peace proposal of mine, I was abused and personally insulted. Mr. Chamberlain, in fact, spat upon me before the eyes of the world…

j. …it was in keeping with our own harmlessness that England took the liberty of some day meeting our peaceful activity with the brutality of the violent egoist.

k. …the outstanding features of Polish Character were cruelty and lack of moral restraint.

The Intensity and frequency of these projections amply justify the diagnosis of paranoid delusion.

5. Ideal-Ego

The ideal-ego, as we define it, is a compound of images engendered in the mind of the subject, which represent what he would like to be; his level of aspiration; his best self at the height of his career; the man reaching the goal of his ambition. The ideal-ego may be the figure of a master criminal or that of a great benefactor or prophet, its exact nature being dependent upon a host of factors stemming from the id, ego, and superego. In Hitler's case it is clear that the ideal-ego is the dominant force of his conscious and unconscious life. We shall discuss, it presently, in connection with his major configuration of drives and sentiments.

B. MAJOR CONFIGURATION OF OVERT DRIVES AND SENTIMENTS

As a rule, it is difficult to demonstrate a clear-cut integration of overt drives and sentiment in an individual; either (1) because the majority of people are not integrated according to a fixed and consistent pattern or; (2) because the configurations, such as they are, are not wholly discernible, important elements being repressed and unconscious to the subject. We use the term orienting thema to include both conscious and unconscious elements. In Hitler's case, however, it is not expedient to make a distinction between the major configurations of overt drives and sentiments and the orienting thema, because the latter has been made explicit in word and deed and is of a relatively consistent and obvious type. Hitler is one of the relatively few men who has largely lived out his fantasy. The main elements of his major configuration are the following:

1. <u>Positive Cathexis * of Power.</u>

Hitler's sentiments in favor of power as opposed to all forms of weakness may be divided into (a) cathexis of powerful nations and (b) cathexis of powerful rulers.

* Positive cathexis = value, attraction, power to evoke love, respect.
* Negative cathexis = the reverses power to evoke aversion, scorn, hate.

(i) <u>Positive cathexis of powerful groups, (nations).</u>

The very first enthusiasm entertained by the boy Hitler was an admiration for Germany. We have already noted his membership in the Nationalist movement as a school boy and listed the determinants of this enthusiasm. The following quotations will illustrate the persistence of this attitude in later life.

a. Hanisch: Hitler always took the Government's part…invariably approved of all such violent methods as necessary for the State's sake.

b. Hitler: In Vienna I continued as I had done before, to follow up all events in Germany with the fiercest enthusiasm, no matter whether political or cultural questions were concerned. With proud admiration I compared the rise of the Reich with the decline of the Austrian State. (M.K. 69-70).

c. Hitler: Prussia, the germ cell of the Reich, was created by resplendent heroism and not by financial operations or commercial affairs, and the Reich itself was in turn only the most glorious reward of political leadership and military death-defying courage. (M.K. 201).

It was Hitler's love of power that attracted him to the history of Great Britain.

d. Hitler: No nation has more carefully prepared its economic conquests with the sword with greater brutality, and defended it later more ruthlessly, than the British. (M.K. 189).

e. Hitler: England did not conquer India by the way of justice and law: she conquered India without regard to the wishes, to the views of the natives or to their formulations of justice; and, when necessary, she has upheld this supremacy with the most, brutal ruthlessness (M.N.O. 103).

Hitler has always admired the ruling classes everywhere as opposed to the underprivileged.

f. Hitler: Our big industrialists have worked their way to the top by reason of their efficiency. In virtue of this selection, which merely proves their higher race, they have a right to lead.

(ii) <u>Positive cathexis of powerful individuals (rulers).</u>

It is difficult to say whether it was the figure of a powerful individual or the vague sense of a powerful class or nation that first excited Hitler's admiration, but certainly in the course of his life there have been a series of heroes who have stirred his enthusiasm and shaped his ego ideal. Among these may be mentioned his teacher of history, Ludwig Poetsch; the fervent anti-Semitic, Georg von Schoenerer; the Viennese mayor, Karl Lueger; Richard Wagner; Frederick the Great; Bismarck; the Kaiser; and Mussolini.

a. Hitler: it infuriated me even more than the Viennese Press…expressed its objections against the German Kaiser…Such things made the blood rush to my head.

b. Hanisch: He said…Wagner was a fighter, there

was more greatness and power in Wagner.

c. Over Hitler's desk hangs a portrait of Frederick the Great, whom, of all Germany's historic characters, Hitler has chosen as his hero.

d. Heiden: Roehm's frank brutal energy seemed to inspire a blissful sense of security in Hitler.

e. Hitler: in those days -- I admit it openly -- I conceived the most profound admiration for the great man…what will rank Mussolini among the great of this earth is the determination not to share Italy with Marxism.

The figure of power admired by Hitler is marked by courage, military valor, brutality and absence of sympathy or compassion. <u>It is characteristic of him to interpret humane feeling as weakness.</u>

2. <u>Need for Deference Toward Power.</u>

Differing from a good many other would-be dictators or revolutionists, Hitler displayed, and still to some extent displays, a marked deference towards his superiors, exhibiting thereby, no doubt, a pattern that he was forced to adopt in the presence of his overbearing father.

(i) Heiden: Subordination he took seriously down to the smallest details: to respect one's superior officers; never to contradict, to submit blindly. Hitler displayed a servile solicitude for the clothes, boots and food of his superior officers.

(ii) Strasser: Hitler's attitude towards the General was obsequious; he was in agreement with everything Ludendorff said.

Hitler and President Hindenburg on the Day of Potsdam, March, 1933

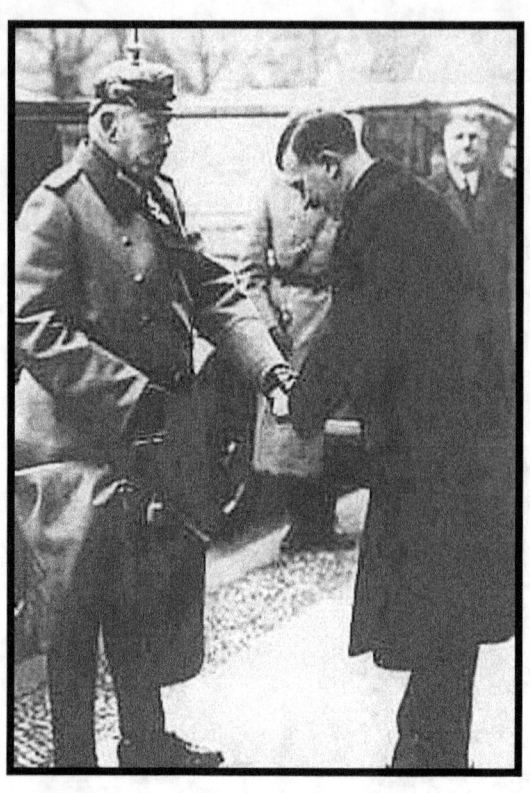

Note the subservience of Hitler's bow.

(iii) Heiden: In the midst of the Munich Putsch, Hitler exclaimed to Kahr in a hoarse voice, "Excellency, I will stand behind you as faithfully as a dog."

(iv) Lamia: in the course of his peroration he came to speak of Generals Ludendorff and von Seeckt; at such moments he stood at attention and trumpeted forth the words "general" and "Excellency." It made no difference that one of the generals was on his side, while the other, von Seeckt, commander-in-chief of the Reichswehr, was his enemy; he abandoned himself entirely to the pleasure of pronouncing the high-sounding titles. He never said "General Seeckt," he said "His Excellency Herr Kolonel General von Seeckt," letting the words melt on his tongue and. savoring their after-taste. At this moment, he was the typical professional sergeant.

3. <u>Negative Cathexis of 'Weakness.</u>

Hitler's sentiments in this category are the natural complement of his high positive cathexis for power. A few illustrations will suffice.

(1) Hitler: A stronger generation will drive out the weaklings, because in its ultimate form the urge to live will again and again break the ridiculous fetters of a so-called "humanity" of the individual, so that its place will be taken by the "humanity" of nature, which destroys weakness in order to give its place to strength,

(ii) Hitler: these upper layers (of intellectuals) lack the necessary will-power. For will-power is always weaker in these secluded, intellectual circles than in the masses of the primitive people.

(iii) Hitler: …the Jewish Christ-Creed with its effeminate pity-ethics. (Rauschning).

(iv) Hitler: Anybody who is such a poltroon that he can't bear the thought of someone nearby having to suffer pain had better join a sewing-circle, but not my party, comrades. (Rauschning).

(v) Hitler: Unless you are prepared to be pitiless, you will get nowhere. Our opponents are not prepared for it, not because they are humane...but because they are too weak. (Rauschning).

4. <u>Ideal-Ego, Powerful Individual.</u>

The process involved here is merely that of the internationalization of the positively cathected, powerful individual described above. What was once external became internal and was accepted as the goal of endeavor. Around this central notion of the powerful individual there has developed an ideology based on the so-called aristocratic principle in nature. The final conception is that of a super superman, leader of a nation of supermen who govern the globe. This notion is deeply imbedded in the German character as a result of; (1) the autocratic position of the father In German family structure; (2) systematic indoctrination in the home and in the schools, and; (3) the position of Germany among the European nations; a powerful community encircled and for a long time eclipsed in power and glory by France and then by Great Britain. The main sources of Hitler's ideology are such men as Carlyle, through his life of Frederick the Great, Gobineau, Wagner, Houston Stewart Chamberlain, Nietzsche and Georges Sorel (Reflections sur la Violence). Not that Hitler read all or even most of these authors but their ideas were transmitted to him through various secondary sources which he read eagerly and took to heart during his years in Vienna. The following quotations give an outline of Hitler's philosophy.

(i) Hitler: …most important precondition in life -- namely, the necessity to be strong. (M.N.O. 625).

(ii) Hitler, quoted, by Rauschning: But fortune follows where there is a firm will.

(iii) Hitler: Always before God and the world. the stronger has the right to carry through what he will. (M.N.O. 50).

(iv) Hitler, quoted by Rauschning: Brutality is respected. Brutality and physical strength. The plain man in the street respects nothing but brutal strength and ruthlessness. (N.B. - This is an excellent example of self- projection and sums up in a nutshell the crux of Hitler's personality.)

(v) Hitler: In the end, only the urge for self-preservation will eternally succeed. Under its pressure, so-called "humanity," as the expression of a mixture of stupidity, cowardice, an imaginary superior intelligence - will melt like snow under the March sun. (M.K. 175).

(vi) Hitler: Every view of life…will remain without importance...unless its principles have become the banner of a fighting movement. (M.K. 575).

(vii) Hitler: Terror is not broken by power of mind but by terror. (M.K. 494-5).

(viii) Hitler: The terror in the workshops, in the factory, in the assembly hall, and on occasions of mass demonstrations will always be accompanied by success as long as it is not met by an equally great force and terror. (M.K. 58)

5. Social Ideal, Powerful Folk.

One will not be able to understand Hitler's personality, its extraordinary force, its maintenance this side of insanity, and its influence on the German people without taking full account of his emotional identification with an ideal Germany as he conceives it, and the dedication of his efforts to the creation of such a Germany. The principles of his program are expressed in the following series of quotations:

(i) Hitler, quoted by Rauachning: There will be a Herren class; an historical class tempered by battle and welded from the most varied elements.

(ii) Hitler…(The Folkish view) feels the obligation in accordance with the Eternal Will that dominates this universe to promote the victory of the better and stronger, and to demand the submission of the worst and the weaker. (M.K. 580).

(iii) Hitler: We recognize that freedom can eternally be only a consequence of power and that the source of power is the will. Consequently, the will to power must be strengthened in a people with passionate ardor. (M.N.O. 24).

(iv) Hitler: His (Youth's) entire education and development has to be directed at giving him the conviction of being absolutely superior to the others. (M.K. 618).

(v) Hitler: The parliamentary principle of decision by majority, by denying the authority of the person and placing in its stead the member of the crowd in question since against the aristocratic idea of Nature. (M.K. 103).

(vi) Hitler: We want to be the supporters of the dictatorship of national reason, of national energy, of national -- brutality and resolution. (M.N.O. 66).

(vii) Hitler quoted by Rauschning; One thing is and remains eternally the same: force. Empires are made by the sword, by superior force -- not by alliances.

What must be pointed out here is; (1) that Hitler came in to Germany as an outsider, (he was not reared in the system); (2) that he started operating with a relatively simple, clear-cut, fanatically held conception of the proper social pattern; (3) that he started with a small nucleus and built a rapidly growing party according to his preconceived social ideal; (4) that this party usurped power and spread to include most of the nation:

(viii) Hitler: The N. S. G. W. P. must not be the masses' slave, but their master! (M.K. 698).

and finally; (5) that Hitler's social ideal is not confined to the German people within the national boundary, but to the German folk or race wherever they are. It is a world dominion that he envisages by people that are constitutionally alike.

What we have here in the simplest terms is the Master-Slave pattern of social relationships to the exclusion of all other patterns. What is most distinctive is not the presence of this idea, which is as old as the history of man, but the absence of other patterns -- the complete substitution of contempt for sympathy.

6. Need for Dominance. Ruthless Will to Power.

Hitler's positive cathecation of a powerful, nation and a powerful ruler has been described, as well as his creation of a social ideal in which Power was to be carried to its furthest point. His deference, even obsequiousness when face to face with representatives of power, has also been described. What we have now to deal with is the problem of the gradual change of emphasis from deference to dominance. We can say, I think, with some justification that if Hitler's ideal social pattern had existed in Germany - that the nation had been under the dictatorship of an iron man - he might have been willing to take his place in the system as a subordinate, just as he did as a corporal in the army; but the fact that such a social pattern was not in operation, stimulated him to inaugurate it. He became dissatisfied with one political leader after another; Kahr, Ludendorff, etc., and by degrees forced himself into the role that, according to his scheme, somebody must fill. It is as if a masochist, finding no one to play a role sufficiently sadistic to gratify his eroticism, were to decide to adopt that role himself. We have to take account here of the possibility of vicarious pleasure in either role. Listening to Hitler's words, we often get a certain sense of his identification with the sadist when he is adopting the submissive role, and his identification with the masochist when he is acting as a brutal tyrant. To explain the identification with the sadist, we must assume an elementary need for dominance, or will to power, which gets satisfied in this roundabout way. Anyhow, it is clear that as time went on during the years after World War I, Hitler's attitude underwent some modification. From the obtrusively submissive corporal he became the obtrusively dominant leader of a party.

(i) Heiden: …(As time went on) he felt himself superior to his recognized superiors. The obedient soldier was transformed into one who knew better; the underling into one who could do things better.

This change was concomitant with Hitler's discovery of his own oratorical powers. He gave way more and more to the demon within him. The ambitious sadist, his infantile belief in omnipotence being reactivated by the hysterical approval of the masses, came into his own. We are dealing here with a personality who enviously admires his enemies. His enemies are those who dominate, oppose and frustrate him with force. He hates the person who embodies this force but he worships the force and as so patterns himself on the object of his hate. This explains why Hitler was attracted to the Marxists and their methods for gaining power.

(ii) Lerner: He went to school not only to the Marxists. He has a great admiration for the organization and methods of the Catholic Church. He speaks again and again of how much he learned by studying the propaganda the British used during the war. And he expresses admiration for American advertising technique.

(iii) Hitler: We had a chance (during World War I) to become acquainted with the incredible discipline of our opponents' propaganda. And still today it is my pride to have found the means for beating, finally, its very makers. Two years later I was master in his craft.

The picture we get here is that of a man who, like a great number of Germans, entertains the conception of an iron man who will save Germany, and wonders, at the same time, whether he himself has the necessary genius to be that iron man. As time went on, Hitler came more and more to identify himself with the hero; but even at the moment that he was approaching the very summit of his power he was overcome with misgivings. Perhaps he was not this superman, but merely the bridge to the superman, as Nietzsche often said of himself.

(iv) Hitler: We are all, in a small way, like St. John, (the Baptist). I wait for Christ!

(v) Hitler, quoted by Rauschning: The new man is among us! He is here! How are you satisfied? I will tell you a secret. I have seen the Vision of the new man -- fearless and formidable. I shrank from him!

(N.B. Here is a suggestion that beyond the exercise of power there is a greater enjoyment -- shrinking before a still greater force.)

7. Identification with Ideal-Ego.

A few quotations will be sufficient to show the extent of Hitler's identification with his own (and the average German's) ideal-ego.

(i) Hitler, quoted by Russell:

Who won the campaign in Poland?
I did;
Who gave the orders?
I did;
Who had all the strategic ideas which made victory possible?
I did;
Who ordered the attack?
Ich, Ich, Ich, Ich...

(ii) Hitler, addressing Schuschnigg, quoted by Fuchs: Do you not realize that you are in the presence of the greatest German ever known to history!

(iii) Hitler: I am one of the hardest men Germany has had for decades, perhaps for centuries, equipped with the greatest authority of any German leader...but above all, I believe in my success. I believe in it unconditionally. (M.N.O. 871).

(iv) Hitler, addressing the Supreme Commanders before the polish campaign, quoted by Lochner:

In the last analysis there are only three great statesmen in the world; Stalin, myself and Mussolini...our strength consists in our speed and in our brutality. Genghis Khan led millions of women and children to slaughter with premeditation and a happy heart. History sees in him solely the founder of a state. It's a matter of indifference to me what a weak western European civilization will say about me. I have issued the command -- and I'll have anybody who utters but one word of criticism executed by a firing squad -- that our war aim does not consist in reaching certain lines, but in the physical destruction of the enemy, accordingly, I have placed my death-head formations in readiness with orders to them to send to death, mercilessly and without compassion, men, women and children of Polish derivation and language.

Hitler sees himself, not only as Germany's greatest strategist and war lord, but also as the chosen instrument of God, the savior .of the German folk, and the founder of a new spiritual era which will endure, as Christ's kingdom was designed to endure, for a thousand years. It is not to be wondered at, therefore, that Hitler has often identified himself with Christ.

(v) Hitler: Therefore, I believe today that I am acting in the sense of the Almighty Creator. By warding off the Jews I am fighting for the Lord's work. (M.K. 84).

Hitler: My feeling as a Christian points me to my Lord and Savior as a fighter. It .points me to the man who once, in loneliness, surrounded by only a few followers, recognized these Jews for what they were and summoned men to the fight against them; and who, God's truth, was greatest, not as a sufferer but as a fighter. In boundless love as a Christian and as a man I read through the passage which tells us how the Lord rose at last in his might and seized the scourge to drive out of the temple the brood of vipers and adders...I recognize more profoundly than ever before the fact that it was for this that He had to shed his blood upon the cross. (M. N. O. 26).

Hitler: When…I see these men standing in their queues…then 1 believe I would be no Christian, but a very devil, if I felt no pity for them; if I did not, as did our Lord two thousand years ago, turn against those by whom today this poor people is plundered and exploited. (M.N.O. 27).

Hitler may very well have realized that he could not make of his physique anything very imposing or resplendent. Perhaps it was an uncanny wisdom on his part that caused him to adopt, or at least retain, the appearance of a typical, lower middle class man. Anyhow, he stands out among others of his type by an adherence to the uniform of a commonplace storm trooper or the vestments of an average citizen. He has not yielded to the temptation of dressing himself up in a fine uniform or in imperial robes as did Napoleon. After the war, he went about in jack-boots swinging a hippopotamus-hide whip, and a plastic surgeon has removed superfluous fat from his nose; and he has studied as consciously as any actor the walk, the gestures and the manner suitable to his position; but still, despite these and many other efforts to create a satisfying visual impression, he has preserved certain modesties that have ingratiated him with certain classes in Germany. According to the legend, he is a humble, ascetic man and this holds, despite the known fact that, in his study at the Berghof, a huge portrait of himself as Fuehrer hangs over him eternally.

8. Need for Aggression, Sadism.

The Marquis de Sade maintained that his cruelties were not inflicted with the purpose of giving others pain, but rather to increase to the utmost his own sense of power; thus, according to his version, aggression was subsidiary to dominance. In Hitler's case, however, although the will to power is the central principle, fitted with it is a vindictiveness which takes pleasure in the painful humiliation of his adversaries. Enough illustrations of the sadism mixed up with Hitler's need for dominance have already been given; we only need to point out here what is known the world over, namely, that his ideology of power has been expressed in definite actions of aggression, particularly against weaker, helpless individuals and groups. Statements such as the following have been the precursors of unprecedented brutality:

(i) Hitler, quoted by, Rauschning: I shall spread terror by the surprise employment of all my measures.

(ii) Hitler, quoted by Heiden: There will be no peace in the land until a body is hanging from every lamp post.

(iii) Hitler, quoted by Rauschning: But even If we could not conquer them, we should drag half the world into destruction with us, and leave no one to triumph over Germany. There will not be another 1918. We shall not surrender.

An account of Hitler's personal aggressiveness against another man is given by Helden:

(iv) (At the Munich Putsch) The first to be arrested was the Standard leader, Count Spreti. The young Count was set in front of Hitler; he made a movement toward his pocket, as though to grasp his pistol. Thereupon Hitler raised his whip, struck Count Spreti on the head with the stout iron-bound end, and threshed him on the face in blind fury until Count Spreti collapsed.

The purge of 1934, the anti-Semitic atrocities, the unspeakable crimes committed in Poland; these and many other actions executed or ordered by Hitler demonstrate the extent of his sadism and revengefulness,

9. Need for Insociation (Collective Identification).

Hitler's psychology cannot be understood if he is considered apart from his identification with the German people, or rather with his ideal for Germany. From the very beginning, we have evidence of his desire to become a member of the Reich, which, to be sure, was more in the nature of a fantasied insociation with a vaguely conceived tradition than it was a desire for relationship with concrete individuals. Until he enlisted in the German Army, there are no definitive instances of his ever belonging to an organized group, unless it was a little Nationalist's Club in school. No doubt this long period of egocentric isolation increased his need for insociatlon. We note that at school he showed tendencies to be an agitator; and Hanish tells us that in Vienna he was continually talking up the idea of forming an association among his flophouse friends for financial or political purposes.

Although in a sense he was a lone wolf (he went by the name of Wolf), it was also true that he had to have followers about him. One of the first things he created was a bodyguard, and the creation of the National Socialist Party was essential to his achievement. Hitler is inconceivable without the masses, but it was not so much the concrete, individual party members whom we have in mind here, rather Hitler's conception of the German Volk, with whom, in his imagination, he was identified. He believed, and the people believed, that he loved Germany; and if Germany is perceived in his terms there is no reason to doubt this dedication. Without this, he would have become a criminal, or lived out his life as a futile and penniless painter of postcards. It was this feeling of oneness with Germany and the fact that he could identify his revengefulness with the need for aggression, latent in the German nation, which enabled him to hold his ground this side of insanity. Once the Party had conquered the German people, he could function corporo-centrically rather than egocentrically. It was this that saved him and won him adherents.

10. Need for Creation (Social).

It was not Germany as it was, or had been, that Hitler represented but rather the ideal social pattern which he wished to impose on the country. Not only during his days of rumination in Vienna, but later it was necessary for him to construct an ideology from diverse sources in terms of which he could preach to the people. None of the elements were original with him but some inventiveness was required in developing the precise combination of principles that became the creed of the Nazi Party. Besides this, he was continually preoccupied with inventing means to his goals, which involved a considerable amount of creative thought; thus, to a certain extent, he functioned as a creative artist and certainly conceived of himself as such.

(i) Hitler: Or must not the task of the leading states-man be seen in the birth of a creative idea or plan in itself, rather than in the ability to make the ingen-uity of his plans understandable to a flock of sheep and empty-heads for the purpose of begging their gracious consent? (M.K. 101-102).

11. Need for Exposition.

Having arrived at his major policy - his ideological goal with its subsidiary aims - it was necessary to communicate these to the people, and so to create a Party, and later a nation, dedicated to the achieve-ment of the determined goal. Here the need for exposition took the form of writing MEIN KAMPF, but more especially the form of speech-making. Hitler is eloquent in stressing the importance of the orator as opposed to the writer when it comes to immediate potency in instigating action. We must certainly rate the need for exposition as maximally strong in Hitler's personality. In boyhood he was already haranguing his schoolmates and his family. Likewise in Vienna and at Company Headquarters during the war, and everlastingly from then on he has continued to make speeches to real or imaginary audiences. His chief function, perhaps, as he conceived it, was to convert the German people to his way of thinking. and thus to create the Germany that he was devoted to in his imagination.

One final point: insociation, creation and exposition were fused by Hitler's conception of himself as mouthpiece of the whole people. He was not creating an individualistic philosophy and imposing it on Germany, but rather, as he saw it, giving voice to the deepest needs and longings of the masses. Here, the editors of MEIN KAMPF have something to say:

(i) The leader is he who most strongly senses the needs and desires of the unified nation, and not he who, as Nietzsche and Stefan George believed, makes use of the "slaves" in order to assure the triumph and happiness of a more regal aristocracy than the world has known; in short, for all his elements of patriotic mysticism, Hitler is no

Platonist, but a Spartan in the simplest sense. That is why Germans have found it so difficult to resist him. As one of them has put it; "He flatters us all into acquiescence." (M.K. Note, 127-8).

In so far.as Hitler conforms to this role, he is egocentric, corporo-centric and ideocentric all at once.

12. Orienting Thema

Much evidence could he brought to bear to demonstrate that Hitler's energies would never have been fully involved if it had not been for Germany's defeat and collapse. Up to that time, he had political convictions, to be sure, hut the sufficient stimulus was lacking. The critical point came, as was mentioned above, when he lay blind in the military hospital and made his vow to reinstate his fallen motherland. Therefore, we would he inclined to put Hitler's orienting thema, the plot of his active striving, in these words: The treacherous, overpowering and contaminating; the weakening and depreciation of a pure and noble object is the tragic spectacle which arouses the hero and incites him to agitate revenge. As Leader and Messiah, he compels the object, by sheer will and eloquence, to adopt a course of ruthless aggression, the goal being to annihilate the contaminator and aggressor, and so, prided by its almighty ruler and redeemer, to become supremely pure, powerful and superior, and thus everlastingly respected. His work done, the hero relinquishes power and dies, revered as the progenitor of an uncorrupted and masterful race that will live on in fulfilment of his word. (N.B.;the elements of purity and contamination will be fully discussed later).

13. Lack of Need Affiliation, Need Nurturance.

Hitler's strong drives for aggressive dominance and self-assertion have been described. These are the features of the man's personality which have attracted and shocked the world, but what is more distinctive, perhaps, is not the presence of these all-too-human tendencies, but the lack of opposing drives which, in normal people, balance and mitigate the evil effects of rampant egocentrism. Hitler has shown extraordinarily little ability to establish and maintain friendships, to adjust himself to the needs and wishes of other people and a minimum of sympathy for human suffering and affliction. Whatever tendencies of this sort he once possessed have been long-since trampled under-foot.

C. MINOR CONFIGURATIONS OF NEEDS AND SENTIMENTS

Hitler is a peculiarly single-minded fanatic and the greater part of his energies have been caught up in the major configuration outlined in the previous section. Anyhow, other configurations and patterns of behavior are of relatively little consequence in a summary analysis of this sort. Suffice it to mention:

1. Need for Sex.

Although the Press has led the German people to believe periodically that Hitler had found the girl he was looking for all these years, a good many close observers have come to the conclusion that he is asexual. It is generally said that Germany is his beloved, his mother and his wife, and that when he addresses the masses, whom he thinks of as feminine, he is courting, appealing to, complaining to and arousing the woman of his heart. That this is not entirely satisfying to his sex instinct will be indicated in a later section.

2. Need for Creation (Architecture).

Hitler's ambitions to become an architect were frustrated by his lack of education and talent, but since he has become supreme ruler of Germany he has given free play to this interest. He has had a part in planning and designing a number of the recent buildings, system of roads, etc. This tendency is only of significance to us in so far as we can infer from the products of his mind certain underlying forces; therefore, we will postpone consideration of this side of his character until a later section.

It should be noted here that Hitler's interest in architecture is very real. It forms an essential ingredient in his system of sentiments. The evidence for this is not limited to his own statements but is furnished by a close study of his metaphors. He speaks of architecture as the queen of the arts. No doubt painting and architecture were connected to some extent with a certain voyeurism, but they also had other significances. The following passage is suggestive of voyeurism:

(i) I had eyes for nothing but the buildings...all day long, from early morn' until late at-night, I ran from one sight to the next, for what attracted me most of all were the buildings. For hours on end I would stand in front of the opera or admire the Parliament Buildings; the entire Ringstrasse affected me like a fairy tale out of the *Arabian Nights*. (M.K. 26-27). In accordance with the conventions of symbolic interpretation, it is possible to conceive of these impressive buildings as psychic equivalents of the mother whom he has lost. We are also reminded, here, of the unique claustrum which Hitler had constructed for himself on the top of the mountain behind his retreat at Berchtesgaden.

D. TYPE OP PERSONALITY STRUCTURE: COUNTERACTIVE NARCISSISM

The drives, sentiments and traits so far listed and discussed; Hitler's high ideal-ego, his pride, his dominance and aggression, and his more or less successful repression of the superego, indicate that his personality structure corresponds to that of counteractive Narcissism. The implication of this term is that the manifest traits and symptoms of Hitler's personality represent a reaction formation to underlying feelings of wounded self-esteem. When one examines systematically the common manifestations of Counteractive Narcissism, one finds that a majority of them are clearly exhibited in Hitler's behavior; therefore, by running over the list of these common characteristics, we can bring together some loose ends and subsume them all under one formulation. Here, we shall not attempt to be exhaustive, but satisfy ourselves with some of the more typical manifestations.

1. Narci-sensitivity: low tolerance of belittlement, depreciation, criticism, contradiction, mockery, failure; inability to take a joke; tendency to harbor grudges; not forgetting and forgiving.

(i) Hanisch: Hitler could never stand any criticism of his paintings.

(ii) Hanisch: Hitler could not stand to be contradicted. He would get furious. He couldn't restrain himself, would scream and fidget with his hands.

(iii) Rauschning: He looked around apprehensively and suspiciously, with searching glances at us. I had the impression that he wanted to see if anyone was laughing.

2. <u>Recognition (Self-Exhibition)</u>: self-display; extravagant demands for attention and applause; vainglory.

(i) Hitler's appearance at meetings and rallies are dramatized to the fullest extent. He is careful to have electric lights shining on him in such a way as to produce the most striking effects possible, etc., etc.. However, one gets the impression the exhibitionism is limited to talking before a crowd, (at which times it is extreme), but that ordinarily he is self-conscious and ill at ease, and does not particularly enjoy showing himself in public, although he must do this to maintain-his power.

3. <u>Autonomy (Freedom)</u>:- self-will to insist on a sufficient area of liberty, on free thought, speech and action. Resistance or defiance in the face of forceful coercion or restraints; to combat tyranny.

(i) It is said that Hitler was unruly as a youth, intolerant of frustration. After his father's death, he was given his own way, and after leaving school became increasingly resistant to rules and regulations. He was never able to hold a job. He wanted to be an artist and live like a Bohemian. We must therefore place him high on this variable although in him it does not take its usual form (defensive individualism). Due to his political ambitions, Hitler needed the alliance of the masses.

(ii) Hitler: The thought of being a slave in an office made me ill; not to be master of my own time, but to force an entire life-time into the filling in of forms. (M.K. 12).

(iii) Heiden: Feder…also said that the Fuehrer must be educated in systematic work. For this purpose he had selected an officer who was to serve Hitler as secretary, to map out the day's work according to the clock and, in general, to introduce order and a program into the Furhrer's activity. When Hitler heard this, he banged his fist on the table and shouted, ''Who do those fellows think they are? I shall go my own way, as I see fit.'' But he accepted the secretary.

4. Dominance (Self-Sufficiency)

When one is in a position of authority, to plan and make decisions without consulting others; to refuse to change an announced decision; to resent disagreements and interference; to be annoyed by opposition; to insist on being sole ruler of one's province -- home, business, political party, nation.

(i) Heiden, quoting Hitler: I am not contending for the favor of the masses...I alone lead the movement and no one can impose conditions on me so long as I personally bear the responsibility. And I once more bear the whole responsibility for everything that occurs in the movement.

5. Refusal of Subordinate Position; to avoid, refuse or leave a position which does not do justice to one's felt powers or accomplishments; to want the first place or nothing (fusion with Autonomy).

(i) Hitler's refusal to accept membership in the Cabinet in 1932. He insisted on complete power.

6. Reluctance to Admit Indebtedness to be disinclined to express gratitude or acknowledge help received, to deny or minimize the contribution of others

(i) Rauschning: Hitler has always been a poseur. He remembers things he has heard and has a faculty of repeating them in such a way that the listener is led to believe that they are his own.

7. Counteractive Achievement.

Persistent efforts in the face of unexpected obstacles; or re-striving after a defeat; or repeated and enduring attempts to overcome fears, anxieties, deficiencies or defects; efforts to defeat a once successful rival.

(i) Heiden: When others, after a defeat, would have gone home despondently, consoling themselves with the philosophic reflection that it was no use contending against adverse circumstances, Hitler delivered a second and a third assault with sullen defiance. When others, after a success, would have become more cautious, because they would not dare put fortune to the proof too often and perhaps exhaust it, Hitler persisted and staked a bigger claim on destiny with every throw.

(ii) The very first condition for such a manner of fight with the weapons of pure force is, and will always be, perseverance...As soon as intermittent force alternates with indulgence, the doctrine to be suppressed will not only recover again and again, but it will be able to draw new values from every persecution...Only in the eternally regular use of force lies the preliminary condition to success. (M.K. 222).

8. Rejection (Verbal Depreciation)

To belittle the worth of others, especially if they be superiors, rivals and potential critics (fusion of verbal Rejection and. Aggression).

(i) Rauschning: Hitler distrusts everyone who tries to explain political economy to him. He believes that the intention is to dupe him, and he makes no secret of his contempt for this branch of science.

(ii) Hitler: My mind was tormented by the question: Are these still human beings, worthy of being part of a great nation? A torturing question it was. (M.K. 54).

(iii) Hitler: ...it brought me internal happiness to realize definitely that the Jew was no German. (M.K. 77).

(iv) Hitler: ...armed in one's mind with confidence in the dear Lord and the unshakeable stupidity of the bourgeois. (M.K.565).

9. <u>Counteractive Aggression</u>: to repay an insult in double measure -- a tooth for a tooth; to revenge an injury; to attack opponents, superiors and frustrators.

(i) <u>Verbal</u>: to accuse, condemn, curse, damn, depreciate or mock an enemy to his face, or behind his back by criticism, slander, subtle undermining of prestige, smear campaigns, etc. There are hundreds of illustrations of this. It is Hitler's conviction that: ''One can only succeed in winning the soul of a people if, apart from a positive fighting of one's own for one's own aims, one also destroys at the same time the supporter of the contrary.'' (M.K. 468).

(ii) <u>Physical</u>: to attack or kill the depreciating, injuring or frustrating object. Purge of 1934; Anti-Semitism; Wars, etc.

10. <u>Intra-deference (Compliance)</u>: obedience to one's own intuitions and impulses; self-trust; fidelity to one's own feelings, sentiments, tastes, judgments, experiences.

(i) Hitler: But I knew, just the same, that my place would be there where my inner voice directed me to go.

(ii) Hitler: Nothing will move me to go another way but the way which experience, insight and foresight tell me to go. (M.N.O. 374). (N.B., Illustrations of this are plentiful; see Id.)

11. <u>Creation and Cathection of an Ideal-ego</u>: satisfaction with one's ideal, with the height of one's aspirations; identification with this ideal.

(i) Many illustrations have been given under ideal-ego and identification with ideal-ego.

12. <u>Ideal-ego Intra-deference (Respect)</u>: self-esteem; satisfaction with conduct, abilities and accomplishments of self.

(i) Although, as I shall attempt to prove, Hitler's character structure is a reaction-formation to tendencies of which he is highly contemptuous, both these tendencies and the contempt are largely unconscious to him. Much more conspicuous in his conscious psychology are his superiority feelings, his self-esteem, his out-flying self-confidence.

(ii) Hitler (at the age of nineteen years): I waited with pride and confidence to learn the result of my entrance examination. I was <u>so convinced of my success</u> that the announcement of my failure came like a bolt from the blue. (M.K. 27).

(iii) Hitler: I devoted myself enthusiastically to my passion for architecture... I was able to read or draw late into the night. I was never tired. Thus my belief that my beautiful dream of the future would become reality, perhaps only after many years, was strengthened. I was <u>firmly convinced</u> that someday I would make a name as an architect. (M.K. 45).

(iv) (Hitler believed himself a man of destiny even while serving as a corporal): in those months, for the first time I felt fully the whims of fortune which kept me at the front in a place where any lucky move on the part of a negro could shoot me down, while somewhere else I would have been able to render a different service to my country. For I was bold enough to believe even then that I would have succeeded in this. (M.K.244).

(v) Hitler addressing Schuschnigg, quoted by Fuchs: Do you not realize that you are in the presence of the greatest German ever known to history!

13. <u>Defendance</u>: to defend one's self-esteem verbally by offering excuses and justifications; by blaming others; by depreciating the judges; by exalting other aspects of one's personality, etc.

Hitler's prime method of defending the status of his self is by blaming others (extra-punitive reaction). Two other common methods are these:

(i) Connecting self with other (respectable or great) people, who have done the same, or had the same happen to them, or suffered from the same defect (n Rec).

Hitler: .If we committed high treason, then count-less others did the same…I deny all guilt so long as I do not find added to our little company those gentlemen who helped... (M.N.O. 80).

(ii) Proclaiming worth of criticized part of self, or another part, or of self as a whole (n Rec): to assert the merit of what others condemn; to balance a defect with an asset; to wipe out a failure by recalling one's successes in this or in some other field.

Hitler: I believe that, as a Nationalist Socialist, I appear in the eyes of many bourgeois democrats as only a wild man. But as a wild man I still believe myself to be a better European…(M.N.O. 404). Throughout the whole of Hitler's spoken and written words are to be found many evidences that he highly approves of the traits attributed to him in this section, and, more than that, advocates their adoption as the preferred pattern of behavior for the whole nation.

Hitler:...if a people is to become free, it needs pride and will-power, defiance, hate - hate and-once again hate. (M.N.O. 49).

14. Insult as stimulus

It is characteristic of the proud counteractive type of personality that his energies are not engaged unless he has been insulted or injured, or imagined himself belittled in some way. Thus the man of this sort will often actively seek such a stimulus. The following quotation illustrates this important principle:

(i) Hitler: If we had been attacked at that time; nay, if one had only laughed at us, we would have been happy in both events. For the depressing thing was neither the one nor the other, but it was only the complete lack of attention we encountered at that time. This was true most of all for my person. (M.K. 490).

.

15. Compulsive Criminality

Having started on a course of revengeful aggression instigated by a real or supposed insult, the individual is often led to act or to plan actions which are opposed by his conscience. Therefore he is compelled, if he is to fulfill his resolution of revenge, to repress his superego. This often results in a condition of mounting unconscious guilt which must be further subdued by a repetition or extension of the criminal behavior in order, as it were, to prove, by the success attending this conduct, that it is favored by fortune and hence right. This is demonstrated in Hitler's case and is an important dynamical principle of his personality. t is necessary for him to commit crimes, more crimes, in order to appease his superego. As soon as successful offensive action becomes impossible, the man will become a victim of a long-repressed superego, a condition which will lead to suicide or mental breakdown.

VI. DYNAMICAL INTERPRETATION OF THE MAJOR CONFIGURATION

A. REVENGEFUL DOMINANCE AS A COUNTER-ACTION TO INSULTED NARCISM.

Almost all psychologists who have analyzed Hitler's personality have interpreted it by referring, among other concepts, to Adler's formula: craving for superiority coming out of unbearable feelings of inferiority. We also agree to this conception with special stress laid upon the press of insult (pounded narcism) and the consequent residual tension of revenge bolted up for years and then finding expression in the Cult of Brutality. Even some of his non-psychological associates reached essentially the same conclusion.

(i) Rauschning: Every conversation, however unimportant, seemed to show that this man was filled with an immeasurable hatred. Hatred of what? It was not easy to say. Almost anything might suddenly inflame his wrath and his hatred. He seemed always to feel the need of something to hate.

(ii) Rauchning: In the harshness and unexampled cynicism of Hitler there is something more than the repressed effect of a hypersensitiveness, which has handicapped its bearer. It is the urge to reprisal and vengeance; a truly Russian, nihilistic feeling.

(iii) Rauschning: Hatred – personal hatred -- rang out in his words; revenge for early years of poverty for disappointed hopes, for a life of deprivation and humiliation.

(iv) Heiden: Anyone acquainted with the unhappy life of this lonely man knows why hatred and. persecution mania guided his first political foot-steps. In his heart he nursed a grudge against the world and he vented it on guilty and innocent alike. His cracking voice, his jerky gait, his sawing gestures expressed a hatred of which all who saw him were conscious.

Hitler has experienced almost all the varieties of press that in our experience are capable of giving rise to wounded narcissism; chiefly the following deserve mention:

1. Physical inferiority: Hitler's youthful frailty and general bodily awkwardness and weakness has already been described.

2. Press of Aggressive Dominance (insult): Knowing something of the character of Alois Hitler, we can safely infer experiences of abasement and humiliation suffered by the son.

3. Press of Rejection: Some evidence for this has already been given, (Section IV), and more will follow.

4. Press of Lack (poverty and low social status): Here we would point especially to the four years of living among the derelicts of Vienna.

5. Press of Failure: The failure to graduate from the Realschule; the failure to pass the examinations of the Academy of Arts; and the failure to make his living in Vienna these and many others were summated to produce feelings of humiliation and inadequacy.

6. Press of Subordinate Office - Success of Rivals: The fact that Hitler was not promoted in the Army beyond the position of corporal and that he must have seen many younger men being advanced above him helped to aggravate his wounded pride.

7. Sexual Inferiority: Perhaps crucial in this whole cluster of debasing press is Hitler's reported inability to have sexual intercourse. This may be due to physical or psychic impotence.

8. Breakdown of Courage: Hitler's war neurosis is a sign of a breakdown of nervous stamina in the face of overwhelming odds, which was probably experienced by him as a humiliation, especially in view of his ego ideal.

(a) Our own hypothetical reconstruction of the traumatic events which led to the feeling of insulted pride would be somewhat as follows:

(i) Abasement and humiliation of the mother as the result of the press of aggressive dominance and insult from the father, leading eventually to the death of the mother. According to our hypothesis the boy Hitler identified with his mother on the lowest level of his nature. This led to the desire for revenge: aggressive dominance and humiliation of the father.

(ii) Press of rejection coming from the father and perhaps to some extent from the mother (birth of younger sibling). This led to the boy's desire for supra-filiation; incorporation in a larger and more powerful group, namely, Germany, and a feeling of superiority (glory) in this fantasied alliance, together with the justification of releasing aggression against his Government, Austria.

(iii) Abasement and humiliation on self as a result of the press-aggressive dominance and insult from his father. This is similar to the trauma in (i) except here it is on his own account entirely.

It led to the same counteractive need for aggressive dominance and vengeance, the goal being humiliation of the father and omnipotence for himself. The death of his father, when he was thirteen years old, and the five subsequent years when he had his mother pretty much to himself may have served to engender the confidence (enjoyed throughout his life) that he would eventually succeed as ruler.

(iv) Humiliation of self in Vienna as the result of press-rejection, press-deprivation and press-aggressive dominance. Since many of the prominent positions in Vienna were held by Jews, some of Hitler's anti-Semitism, as well as his hatred of Vienna, can be attributed to humiliations received from the upper classes during these years. These wounds to pride helped to augment the mounting residual tension of aggressive dominance. Later, his acceptance as a soldier in the German Army served to relieve his painful feelings and give him feelings of exultation similar to those experienced when he joined the Nationalist's Club as a boy.

(v) Humiliation of self (war neurosis) concomitant with the humiliation and abasement of his motherland as the result of press-aggressive dominance and insult (Versailles Treaty) at the hands of the Allies. As in the previous four cases, this led to the need for aggressive dominance with the aim of reinstating the power and glory of Germany and wreaking vengeance on the Allies.

The hypothesis of identification with the mother on a physical, erotic level calls for the assumption of a strain of femininity in Hitler, combined with a trend of passive homosexuality, and for this we must now list the evidence.

1. Femininity - Passive Homosexuality - Masochism

(a) The feminine component in Hitler's physical constitution had already been described.

(i) Feminine traits. Hitler's sentimentality, his emotionality, his shrieking at the climax of his speeches, his artistic inclinations, his sudden collapses, his occasional softness; these are all typical, not so much of a woman as of a woman in a man.

(ii) Identification with mother. Hitler's belief that he is going to die of cancer as did his mother is suggestive of an underlying empathic relationship.

(iii) Abasement to superiors and strong males. Instances of exaggerated submissiveness to powerful superiors have already been listed.

(iv) Cathexis of male symbols. Hitler has a special liking for a multiplicity of tall, conspicuous columns in architecture and for paintings of stallions (they must never be mares).

(v) Attraction to homosexuals followed by their murder. It is known that Hitler had a special admiration for Roehm; whether it was this individual or Hitler himself who was chiefly responsible in attracting such a large proportion of homosexuals to the Nazi Party is uncertain; but it is known that after two or three months of anxiety and delusions to the effect that Roehm and his fellow homosexuals were plotting to usurp power, Hitler had them all murdered in the purge of 1934.

(vi) Homosexual panic. Some of the nightmares described by several informants are very suggestive of homosexual panic.

Rauschning: Hitler wakes at night with convulsive shrieks. He shouts for help. He sits on the edge of his bed, as if unable to stir. He shakes with fear, making the whole bed vibrate. He shouts confused, unintelligible phrases. He gasps, as if imagining himself to be suffocating. ..Hitler stood swaying in his room, looking wildly about him. "He! He! He's been here!" he gasped. His lips were blue. Sweat streamed down his face. Suddenly, he began to reel off figures, odd words and broken phrases, entirely devoid of sense...then he suddenly broke out, "There, there! In the corner. Who's that?" He stamped and shrieked in the familiar way...

A number of metaphors used by Hitler – images of being stabbed in the rear - recur in his writings.

(vii) Hitler: The development has shown that the people who stab with stilettos in Germany are more powerful than before.

(viii) Hitler: Slowly the fear of the Marxist weapon of Jewry sinks into the brains and souls of decent people like a nightmare. (M.K. 447).

(ix) Hitler: One begins to tremble before the terrible enemy, and thus one has become his final victim. (M.K. 447).

(x) Hitler: There can never be unity between those who manned the walls in the hour of danger, and those who in the last moment pushed the stiletto into their backs.

(xi) Hitler: God be thanked, this is just the meaning of Germanic democracy; that no unworthy climber or moral shirker can come in the back way to rule his fellow citizens...but, should, nevertheless, such a fellow try to sneak in, then he will be easily found out and ruthlessly rebuffed. Out with you, cowardly wretch! Step back, you are soiling the steps; the front stairs leading to the Pantheon of History is not for sneaks but for heroes. (M.K. 117).

Pertinent at this point, perhaps, is Hitler's fear of being poisoned by some deadly powder sprinkled on his bedclothes; as was shown on his visit to Rome and at other times, his bed must be made up by a woman in a particular way, never by a man.

(b) <u>Need for abasement</u>: Hitler's exaggerated submissiveness has been described (B,1 (ii), but a few more notable quotations should be added to transmit the passion that sometimes accompanies this tendency in Hitler. They are all strongly suggestive of <u>masochism</u>.

(i) Hitler, quoted by Rauschning: The plain man in the street respects nothing but brutal strength and ruthlessness -- women, too, for that matter -- women and children. They need wholesome fear. They want to fear something. They want someone to frighten them and make them shudderingly submissive.

(ii) Hitler, quoted by Rauschning: I have seen the vision of the new man, fearless and formidable. I shrank from him.

(iii) Hitler: Like a woman, whose psychic feeling is influenced, less by abstract reasoning than by an undefinable, sentimental longing for complementary strength, who will submit to the strong man rather than dominate the weakling -- thus the masses love the ruler rather than the suppliant. (M.K.56).

(N.B. Another excellent example of projection of self).

(iv) Hitler: He who would win the great masses must know the key which opens the door to their hearts. Its name is not objectivity - that is, weakness - but will power and strength. (M.K. 458).

Hitler has a peculiar habit of falling to the ground suddenly when faced by a critical situation or insurmountable frustration. He does not struggle persistently until he is completely overpowered, but he makes an enormous show of strength, and, when he sees the odds are against him unexpectedly collapses.

Together with these critical abasements, we might include the intra-ggressive tendencies; his preoccupation with suicide and death.

(c) <u>Cathexis for Hitler Youth.</u>

(i) Hitler, quoted by Rauschning: But my magnificent youngsters! Are there finer ones anywhere in the world? Look at these young men and boys. What material! With them I can make a new world

(ii) Hitler how did the eyes of my boys (Hitler youth) shine when I made clear to them the necessity of their mission, (M.K. 729).

(iii) Hitler: …vanity in a beautiful, well-shaped body (to be encouraged by men wearing less concealing clothes).

It is reported by Rauschning that Hitler has had overt homosexual relations and in this connection has mentioned three lovers; one, Forster (Gauleiter of Danzig).

II. Repression of Femininity. Counter-action by Identification with Powerful Male Ideal-ego.

The ruthless aggressiveness of Hitler is the trait which first strikes the eyes of the whole world, but it is not the healthy aggressiveness of a full-blooded, male animal, but a reaction-formation to the tendencies which we have subsumed under inferiority; femininity; passive homosexuality. Hitler's aggressiveness is the compulsive, frantic hate of a neurotic for some un-revenged insult of infancy. The varieties of expressions of this vindictive will to power have already been fully listed. There remains only to be mentioned the many indications that we have of an intense and unrelenting self-contempt which has caused him to admire what he is not - the very opposite of himself.

III. Need for Intra-Rejection (Self-Contempt).

Under the heading *Projections*, we enumerated many instances of where Hitler attributed the traits of his inferior and rejected self to external objects. All of these, and there were many of them, might be cited as evidences of self-contempt, since they represent refusals to acknowledge aspects of himself. Here, we have to call attention to the opposite tendency, namely, that of praising the antithesis of what he is or has been in reality.

(a) Hitler has talked incessantly of superiority of breed. He has praised the aristocracy as the noble result of the process of natural selection -- the nobility were the superior race. He, in contrast, was born of lowly stock, several members of his family being mentally retarded, one feeble-minded. His mother was a simple peasant and domestic servant, and his father an illegitimate son who begot an illegitimate child.

(b) Hitler has scarcely one of the attributes which his own experts ascribe to the Nordic race, and he could never become a member of his own elite guard; and yet he says; "Strong and handsome must my young men be. I will have them fully trained in all physical exercises. I intend to have an athletic youth -- that is the first and chief thing."

Note that Hitler has never had the slightest aptitude for athletics.

(c) Hitler is unmarried and has no children, and yet he preaches increase of population, the sanctity of the family and the necessity of bearing more and more Germans.

(d) Hitler's own life is one of individualistic anarchy -- self-willed and disorderly -- and yet he preaches ''my new order" and demands punctilious discipline from his subordinates.

All these contrasts, and there are many more of them, are pitiful demonstrations of Hitler's self-loathing and as such clinch the diagnosis that we have outlined here. The nearest to a recorded confession of his own self-contempt that has ever come to us is a statement of Hitler's reported by Rauschning:

(i) "I am beginning with the young. We older ones are used up. Yes, we are old already. We are rotten to the marrow...we are cowardly and sentimental. We are beaming the burden of a humiliating past

and have in our blood the dull recollection of
serfdom and servility. But, my magnificent
youngsters"…etc.

(ii) The uninitiated but pure man is tempted to
abandon himself in Klingsor's magic garden, to the
lusts and excesses of corrupt civilization, instead of
joining the elite knights who guard the secret of life,
of pure blood... all of us are suffering from the
ailment of mixed, corrupt blood. How can we purify
ourselves and make atonement and then mount the
steps of a new nobility?"

IV. Negative Cathexis of the Jewish Race.

This is as good a place as any to mention Hitler's
Anti-Semitism and to list what seems to have been,
in his case, the chief determinants of this sentiment:

1. The influence of a number of political thinkers
and speakers whom he admired: Lueger, Feder,
Eckart, etc.

2. His repressed hatred and the need to find an
object on which to vent it: the suitability of the Jew
as a scapegoat because he does not fight with fists
and weapons.

3. The suitability of the Jew as an object on which to project his own repudiated background and traits: his Jewish godfather, (and possibly his Jewish grandfather); his physical timidity and sensitiveness; his polymorphous sexual impulses.

4. The recognition that the repressed aggression in the German people after the Versailles Treaty required a scape-goat -- condemnation of the Jew as good political strategy.

5. The realization, after having once embarked on the road to militarism, that the stirred-up aggression of his followers needed some outlet -- a warming up period -- during the years they had to wait before they were strong enough to declare war on a foreign power. Directing aggression against a common enemy would greatly diminish the likelihood of its being turned against himself.

6. The intensity of his Anti-Semitism is partly accounted for by one of his principles of political action: focus and hostility on a single enemy at a time.

7. In building his military machine, the anti-militaristic Jewish people could not be of much help to him. At its bottom, Fascism is the advocacy of the aggressive drive over and above the acquisitive drive (with which the Jew has generally been identified); and, by the same token, it is the substitution of Power and Glory for Peace and Prosperity; a materialistic paradise on earth (with which Communism and the Jew have also been identified). Finally, the Nazi doctrine of fanatical irrationality (thinking with the blood) is antipathetic to the intellectual relativism of the Jew. Thus, there are several fundamental points of opposition (as well as certain points of kinship) between Nazi ideology and Jewish ideology.

VI. SECTIONS B, C, D, E. - DEVELOPMENT OF HITLER'S SEX COMPLEXES

(Omitted from this edition)

By careful study of the three thousand metaphors that are found in MEIN KAMPF, it was possible to work out the chief patterns of Hitler's emotional and perverse sexual complexes. The conclusions reached by the use of this method were later verified in a conversation with a man who has questioned two of the women with whom Hitler has had relations. There were no discrepancies between the conclusions reached here and those first-hand reports. Although the discovery of these sexual patterns is helpful to a psychiatrist in arriving at a complete formulation of Hitler's character, and therefore indirectly pertinent to the final diagnosis and the predictions of his behavior, it has no bearing on the political situation. Consequently, the sections dealing with this aspect of his personality have been omitted.

VII. ABILITIES AND PRINCIPLES OF ACTION

Hitler has a number of unusual abilities of which his opponents should not be ignorant. Not only is it important to justly appraise the strength of an enemy, but it is well to know whether or not he possesses capacities and techniques which can be appropriated to good advantage. Hitler's chief abilities, realizations and principles of action as a political figure, all of which involve an uncanny knowledge of the psychology of the average man, are briefly these:

1. <u>Full appreciation of the importance of the masses in the success of any movement.</u>

Two quotations might serve to bring out this point.

(i) Hitler: The lack of knowledge of the internal driving forces of great changes led to an insufficient evaluation of the importance of the great masses of the people; from this resulted the scanty interest in the social question -- the deficient and insufficient courting of the soul of the nation's lower classes...(M.K. 138).

(ii) Heiden speaks of, "Hitler's frequently noted incapacity to impose his will in a small circle, and his consummate skill in winning over a crowd prepared by publicity and stage management; and then, with its aid, vanquishing the small circle, too."

2. <u>Recognition of the inestimable value of winning the support of youth</u>.

Realization of the immense momentum given a social movement by the wild fervor and enthusiasm of young men and women. Here we must also include the importance of early training and indoctrination.

3. <u>An identification, through feeling, with the deepest needs and sentiments of the average German and the ability to give passionate expression to these longings.</u>

4. <u>Capacity to appeal to the most primitive, as well as the most ideal, inclinations in man -- to arouse the basest instincts and yet cloak them with nobility; justifying all actions as means to the attainment of an ideal goal.</u> Hitler has seen that men will not combine and dedicate themselves to a common purpose unless this purpose be an ideal one capable of survival beyond their generation. He has perceived also that, although men will die only for an ideal, their continued zest and enterprise can be maintained only by a succession of more immediate and earthly satisfactions.

5. <u>Appreciation of the fact that the masses are as hungry for a sustaining ideology in political action as they are for daily bread</u>. It is with the masses that religious belief has taken root and maintained itself, and in the last decades the ideologies of communism and fascism have also flourished among the common people. It is an error to believe, as many democratic leaders do, that the average man cannot understand and cares nothing for political philosophy. Hitler is most specific on this point, two quotations from his writings being particularly pertinent.

(i) All force which does not spring from a firm spiritual foundation will be hesitating and uncertain. It lacks the stability which can only rest on a fanatical view of life. (M.K. 222).

(ii) Every attempt at fighting a view of life by means of force will finally fail, unless the fight against it represents the form of an attack for the sake of a new .spiritual direction. Only in the struggle of two views of life with each other can the weapon of brute force, used continuously and ruthlessly, bring about the decision in favor of the side it supports. (M.K. 223).

6. <u>The ability to analyze complex social conditions into a few dominant human forces</u>: Hitler is speaking the truth when he says,"1 have the gift of reducing all problems to their simplest foundations…A gift for tracing back all theories to their roots in reality." He has the ability, Rauschning tells us, "of breaking through the wall of prejudices and conventional theories of the experts, and in so doing, he has frequently discovered amazing truths."

7. <u>The ability to portray conflicting human forces in vivid, concrete imagery that is understandable and moving to the ordinary man.</u> This comes down to the use of metaphors in the form of imagery which, as Aristotle has said, is the most powerful force on earth. Public speakers of recent years seem to have overlooked the importance of this principle, relying more on the marshalling of cold, objective facts and figures.

8. <u>The ability to draw on the traditions of the peoples and, by reference to the great classical</u>

mythological themes, evoke the deepest unconscious emotions in his audience. The fact that the unconscious mind is more intensely affected by the great eternal symbols and themes, (that it naturally thinks in these terms,) is not generally understood by speakers and writers. Undoubted-ly in Hitler's case the permeability of his ego to unconscious processes has made this form of utterance more natural than it would be for others.

9. Realization that enthusiastic political action does not take place if the emotions are not involved. Hitler has always insisted that he was bringing about a veritable conversion in the personalities of his adherents rather than a mere intellectual agreement with his views.

10. Realization of the importance of artistry and dramatic intensity in the conductance of large meetings, rallies and festivals. This involves not only an appreciation of what the artist -- the writer, musician and painter -- can accomplish in the way of evoking popular support, but also the leader's recognition of the necessity of his participation in the total dramatic effect as chief character and hero. Thus Hitler has become master of all the arts of highlighting his own role in the movement for a greater Germany. Democratic leaders, on the other hand, disregarding the fact that the artist is trained, above all others, to animate the human spirit, have disregarded this important aspect of life.

11. <u>The ability to appeal to the sympathetic concern and protectiveness of his people</u>; to represent himself as the bearer of their burdens and their future with the result that many people, particularly the women, feel tenderly and compassionately about him, being always careful to avoid inflicting undue annoyance or suffering onto their leader. The intense loyalty of Hitler's Body Guard is an illustration of this protectiveness.

12. <u>Dedication to his mission</u>. This most essential of all of Hitler's characteristics should perhaps have been mentioned first. What is involved here is an intense and profound insociation with the German people, or at least with his vision of what the German people might become. All close observers have agreed that Hitler is sincere in this feeling, and whether this is strictly true or not, he has succeeded in convincing his people that he is a passionate and devoted patriot. It is the spectacle of his far-seeing, dedicated vision and firm, dedicated utterances which arouse the selfless energies of his followers. Citizens of democratic countries who have been brought up in the tradition of extreme individualism cannot readily appreciate this submission of the leader to a social purpose. They are naturally skeptical of Hitler's sincerity and believe that it is forced and artificial. I submit, on the contrary, that it is this insociation, as we have stressed above, which is responsible for the maintenance of Hitler's partial sanity, despite the presence of neurotic and psychotic trends.

13. <u>Self-confidence and sense of infallibility</u>. This might have been detrimental to Hitler's popularity if his decisions had often met with failure, but in as much as his rise to power was almost phenomenal, and events proved that he was so often right in his predictions, his claim to infallibility was accepted and his word was eventually reverenced as a divine pronouncement.

14. <u>Fanatical stubbornness in his adherence to a few principles and to one common goal.</u>

(i) Hitler, quoted by Deuel: Only a storm of glowing passion can turn the destinies of nations, but this passion can only be roused by a man who carries it within himself.

(ii) ...the forceful impression of great overwhelming viewpoints...the convincing force of unconditional belief in them. (M.K. 570).

15. <u>Mastery of the art of political organization.</u>
Here, undoubtedly, Hitler was assisted by several of his shrewder associates; but his own judgment in matters of organization was usually influential above that of all the others.

16. <u>Ability to surround himself with devoted aides whose talents complement his own</u>. In many respects Hitler is deficient, especially in the practices of orderly administration, but he was capable of finding sufficient skill among his adherents and make them work for him regardless of their failings in other respects.

17. <u>Hitler is unusual in history in his conception of the leader as a creator of social forms.</u> Holding this view, it is natural that he should conduct his life at certain seasons as an artist does -- seeking rest and seclusion and waiting for the vision or plan to develop in his subconscious. What other politicians refer to as his bohemianism -- his disorderly and romantic style of life -- is very comparable to the pattern which authors have found most effective in the production of their works. Temperamentally, indeed, Hitler is the arch-romantic. One might suppose that this way of governing one's life has no place in politics, but without question in this instance many of the startling innovations introduced by the Nazis are the results of Hitler's reliance upon the creative imagination directed toward social issues.

18. <u>Most of the world will concede that Hitler has tactical genius</u>. The particular feature that has impressed most observers has been his uncannily precise timing of decisions and actions. As Thyssen has put it; "Sometime his intelligence is astonishing…miraculous political intuition, devoid of all moral sense but extraordinarily precise. Even in a very complex situation he discerns what is possible and what is not."

19. <u>The fact that Hitler has repudiated the operation of conscience in arriving at political decisions</u> has eliminated once and for all the force which checks and complicates the forward-going thoughts and resolutions of most socially responsible statesmen. Thus, Hitler's course is immensely simplified since it is not incumbent upon him to respect the dictates of conscience and so reject a path of action which appeals to him as being most effective. Other statesmen, on the contrary, must either renounce certain programs or pull their punches.

20. <u>Hitler has boasted that he learned the use of terror from the communists and employed it with more effectiveness than his instructors</u>.

21. <u>Mastery of the art of propaganda</u>. This has consisted in the following of certain rules such as; never to admit a fault or wrong; never to accept blame; concentrate on one enemy at a time; blame that enemy for everything that goes wrong; take advantage of every opportunity to raise a political whirlwind.

Many of the specific abilities listed above are exercised as part and parcel of his quite unusual power as a popular orator. So much has been written about Hitler's ability to galvanize an audience by his gestures -- the cadence of his sentences, the resoluteness of his declarations, the passion of his appeals -- that any further description here would be superfluous. It is clear that Hitler becomes transported during a speech and exhibits a personality that is kept in the background at other times. When face to face with his public he becomes a clairvoyant shaman in a trance, as he relinquishes normal controls and allows his emotions full sway.

PREDICTIONS

I shall assume that, from now on the Allied Nations will be closing in on Germany; that Hitler will be confronted by an increasing number of military setbacks in the field, by the devastation of one industrial center after another, and by the spread of a defeatist spirit among the civilian population. How will be behave? There are various possibilities, some of which are more or less desirable, others more or less undesirable, from the Allied standpoint. It is possible, however, that some .of the less desirable final acts of his career may be prevented. The chief possibilities are these:

1. <u>Hitler's behavior will become increasingly neurotic</u>: His capacity to make correct decisions, to devise effective strategy, to encourage his people will diminish steadily. For eight months there have been signs of such a breakdown of psychic strength. Hitler has not appeared and spoken in public at customary occasions; or, if he has spoken, his words have lacked confidence and sustaining value. Several times there have been rumors that he had retired to Berchtesgaden, the victim of nervous illness. Whether this is true or not, it can he certainly predicted that Hitler will experience an increasing number of hysterical seizures in which he will pace and stamp the floor, shriek with rage and eventually collapse in tears. He will seek the solitude of his refuge in the mountains where he will be tormented by dreadful nightmares and melancholia, and become inert. Then, after a period of recuperation, he will arrive at a new plan of aggressive offense. If his military staff are opposed to it, he will assume command himself and lead his troops on another desperate assault against the Russian lines. If unsuccessful, he will have more nervous seizures, relinquish command and again retreat to Berchtesgaden. Hitler has no capacity for sustained defense.

He will speak less and less in public because he cannot face his people if his star is not ascending. He can speak only when he anticipates progress or after a victory. The Russians have shattered Hitler's confidence; and without confidence he is paralyzed. If he stood before his followers now he would probably weep.

Without doubt he will become increasingly fearful of being poisoned, betrayed or shot. Whatever else happens, the above course of events will almost certainly occur. Hitler will become less and less of a leader; others will take over. On the one hand, the military staff. On the other, Himmler, Ribbentrop, Goering, Goebbels, Forster and Koch. There will be dissensions between the Army and the Party, as well as between the Party leaders. But the people will be kept ignorant as long as possible of Hitler's failing nerves, and they will not easily lose their faith in him. Furthermore, he will always reserve and exercise the right to step in at any moment and dictate what shall be done. Thus we can expect to hear nothing of him for a while and then suddenly he will appear unheralded at some spot and something new will happen.

2. <u>Hitler may go insane</u>: He has the make-up of a paranoid schizophrenic, and the load of frustration and failure that is coming to him may crack his resistance, causing him to yield his will to the turbulent forces of his unconscious. This is not undesirable because, even if the truth be kept hidden from the people, the greatest source of strength in Germany will be removed from the scene of action, and morale will rapidly deteriorate as rumors spread. Furthermore, the Legend of the Hero will be severely damaged by such an outcome. There is no good historical instance of the deification of a military or political leader who was defeated and went insane. Finally, if Hitler became insane, he would probably fall into the hands of the Allied Nations; and this, as I shall argue, would be the most desirable possible outcome.

3. <u>Hitler may get killed in battle</u>: At a critical moment, Hitler may decide to lead his elite troops against the Russians, exposing himself so that he will get killed, and so live in the hearts of his countrymen as a valiant hero. He is very likely to choose this course; most undesirable from our Allied point of view. It is undesirable, first, because his death will serve as an example to all his followers to fight with fanatical death-defying energy to the bitter end; and second, because it will insure Hitler's immortality -- the Siegfried who led the Aryan hosts against Bolshevism and the Slav.

4. <u>Hitler may be killed by a German</u>: Hitler is most efficiently protected and it is not likely that anyone shall willfully attempt to kill him. But he may contrive to have someone -- a half-crazy paranoid like himself, instigated to do the deed at some pre-arranged moment when he purposely exposes his person in public. If he could arrange to have a Jew kill him, then he could die in the belief that his fellow countrymen will rise in their wrath and massacre every remaining Jew in Germany. Thus, he would get his ultimate revenge. This would be the most dastardly plan of all, and the most undesirable. It would increase the fanaticism of the soldiers and create a Legend in conformity with the ancient pattern -- Siegfried stabbed in the back by Hagan; Caesar by Brutus; Christ betrayed by Judas, except that here the murderer would not be a close follower. However, it is just possible that Hitler could persuade the beloved Förster to kill him.

5. <u>Hitler may commit suicide</u>: Hitler has often vowed that he would commit suicide if his plans miscarried; but if he chooses this course he will do it at the last moment and in the most dramatic possible manner. He will retreat, let us say, to the impregnable little fortress he has built for himself on the top of the mountain beyond the Berghof (Berchtesgaden). There alone he will wait until troops come to take him prisoner. As a climax, he will blow up the mountain and himself with dynamite, or make a funeral pyre of his retreat and throw himself on it (a suitable Götterdamerung) or kill, himself with a silver bullet (as did the Emperor Christophe); or possibly throw himself off the parapet. This is not at all unlikely. For us it would be an undesirable outcome.

6. Hitler may seek refuge in a neutral country: It is not likely that Hitler, concerned as he is with his immortality on earth, would take so cowardly a course. But one of his followers might drug him and take him in a plane bound to Switzerland, and then persuade him that he should stay there to write his long-planned Bible for the Germanic folk. Since the hero's desertion of his people would considerably damage the Legend, this outcome would be much better that either 3 or 4.

7. Hitler may die: There is no reason to believe that Hitler will die of natural causes in the next three or four years, but he might poison himself and have it announced that he had died of cancer of the stomach or some other incurable illness. This outcome would be natural.

8. <u>Hitler may be seized by the military command or by a revolutionary faction in Germany before the end of the war and immured in some prison fortress</u>.

This event is difficult to envisage from, what we surmise and have been told of the popularity of the man, and the protection afforded him, but if it were to transpire, it would put an ignominious end to the myth of the invincible leader and eventually deliver him into our hands.

9. <u>Hitler may fall into our hands before or after the Germans have surrendered</u>: This would be the next most desirable outcome after number 8 but is perhaps the least likely.

SECTION IV

<u>Predictions of Hitler's Behavior in the Coming Future</u>

(See Section I, Part B)

SECTION V

Suggestions for the Treatment of Hitler Now and After Germany's Surrender

(See Section-I, Part C)

SECTION VI
Suggestions for the Treatment of Germany

(See Section I, Part D)